DIALOGUE IN THE GRECO-ROMAN WORLD

DIALOGUE
IN THE
GRECO-ROMAN
WORLD

LESLIE KELLY

Westphalia Press
An Imprint of the Policy Studies Organization
Washington, DC
2017

DIALOGUE IN THE GRECO-ROMAN WORLD
All Rights Reserved © 2017 by Policy Studies Organization

Westphalia Press
An imprint of Policy Studies Organization
1527 New Hampshire Ave., NW
Washington, D.C. 20036
info@ipsonet.org

ISBN-10: 1-63391-554-9
ISBN-13: 978-1-63391-554-1

Cover and interior design by Jeffrey Barnes
jbarnesbook.design

Daniel Gutierrez-Sandoval, Executive Director
PSO and Westphalia Press

Updated material and comments on this edition
can be found at the Westphalia Press website:
www.westphaliapress.org

Acknowledgments

I would like to thank my parents, Jerry and Nancy Kelly, for their encouragement and support, as well as American Public University's Dr. Vernon C. Smith, Senior Vice President and Provost; Dr. Grace Glass, Dean, School of Arts & Humanities; and Dr. Richard Hines, Director of History and Military History Programs.

TABLE OF CONTENTS

INTRODUCTION

Plato's *Republic* outlines the constitution and conventions for an ideal society. In Book 5 of the *Republic* we are presented with arguments in favor of including women among the guardians of the city. Students of Greek history are sometimes unsure what to make of this. Socrates argues eloquently for the essential equality of men and women, a notion that seems very modern yet which is being propounded here by one of antiquity's most prominent thinkers. Is the true purpose of this discussion to prompt the reader to reflect on the tyranny of convention? Or the true function of government? How should this work influence our understanding of gender in ancient Greece? To answer such questions we must first decide how singular the views expressed here really were. That is, does Plato represent an exception, merely one lone voice among a very small subsection of society (philosophers) who were interested in and capable of examining the role of women in society objectively, without making *a priori* assumptions as to their nature and abilities?

If we look for parallels, we do find that the topic of women's capacity to rule appears in Greek literature composed around or before the date of Plato's dialogue (composed ~380 BCE). Aristophanes' *Assemblywomen* (*Ecclesiazusae*; dates to 391 BCE) included a comic reflection on women's capacity to rule (lines 590–710) as well as the common possession of wives (lines 611–634), also taken up by Plato in Book 5 in the *Republic* And it is believed that both Plato and Aristophanes were engaging with ideas that had already been expressed in a late fifth- or early fourth-century source.[1]

Finding predecessors and/or contemporaries who reflect the same themes shapes our understanding of Plato's work. We see that in

---

1   Andrea Wilson Nightingale, *Genres in Dialogue: Plato and the Construct of Philosophy* (Cambridge: Cambridge University Press, 1995), 177.

this dialogue Plato is taking part in an ongoing conversation about women. If we wanted now to uncover what he is contributing to that conversation we would need to analyze the dialogue with respect to its overall purpose and consider how the passages on women relate to the overall aim of the work. This is where the conventions of the genre of "dialogue" come into play.

In everyday language, the term "dialogue" refers to a conversation between two or more people. In literary terms, the definition of "dialogue" is much more difficult to pin down. Broadly speaking, a literary work will be labeled a dialogue if the work, or a significant portion of it, depicts a conversation taking place between two or more persons in which a specific topic or topics are examined or threshed out. This can take place in the form of a debate or in the form of a series of questions (presented by "interlocutors"—those who ask questions) and answers. The designation "dialogue" was loosely used in antiquity and if we were to try and list all of the dialogues that were produced in the Greco-Roman world, the list would no doubt vary from scholar to scholar. Regardless of this vagueness as to definition, scholars still agree that the genre of dialogue is an important one. By even the narrowest definition they add up to a substantial total and some dialogues are among the most central texts in the classical or early Judeo–Christian canon. Plato's Socratic dialogues show us Greek philosophy at work; in Cicero's dialogues we witness the development of a Roman stance on philosophy, law, religion, and statesmanship; in the dialogues of Justin Martyr, Octavius Felix, and Methodius Christians define their community over against those of Jews and pagans.

Texts, then as now, belong to different categories of writing, the two most significant being fiction and nonfiction. Within this broad categorization there are many different subcategories or genres (novels or short stories in fiction for example or textbooks and journal articles in nonfiction). Different types of texts come with their own set of rules as to how they should be read. Our expectations for a novel differ from the expectations we bring to a nonfiction book; we know that an autobiography gives us a firsthand view and a biography a secondhand view; a textbook offers academic information and a coffee-table book light entertainment. But it is not only the case that different types of books give us different types of information. We read these texts differently, too. When we take up a textbook we (if we are good students) plan to pay attention to chapter headings and to the guiding questions in the margins. These are clues that indicate important points we should think about as we read. Such expectations guide our reading process. Genre in antiquity worked in similar ways: when an ancient Greek read epic poetry he understood that it would provide information about the world of gods and heroes, that it would come in verse form, that it would use metaphorical language. Plutarch, for instance, has an entire work on how to read poetry; Cicero, *Laws* 1.4–5 discusses the different ways of reading poetry and history. In short, the ancient reader would come to an epic poem as an experienced reader of myth and that would form his expectations as a reader.

This book will explain the origins of dialogue in ancient Greece and explain how dialogues of the Greco-Roman world are intended to be read. It will trace key developments in the genre and examine specific significant examples. The historical context of these dialogues will be considered and the issues that need to be taken into account as one uses these sources to help reconstruct or understand the past.

This book has two foci: the first: to address the following questions: What were readers expected to do with these dialogues? How were they to read them? What were the rules of reading them? The second follows from this: given the first points, what difference does it make to us today as students or historians of ancient history? If we want to use these ancient dialogues as evidence how may we responsibly do this given the former?

In what follows I will show you how to approach the reading of any dialogue generically using a basic checklist. Each chapter takes up in succession a major period for dialogue production. The chapter will provide a brief overview of what was produced in that age and discuss any developments in genre conventions. Then a sample dialogue will be analyzed with respect to the checklist and with respect to interpretations of that dialogue in recent scholarship. Applying these two elements (checklist and recent interpretations), conclusions will be drawn so as to demonstrate how we might reconstruct social and political information from the dialogue.

The following list is not exhaustive and some of these points will be more important than others for any given dialogue.[2] It represents a baseline of things to consider before using a dialogue to study the past.

Checklist:

Audience: the intended reader

Frame: the dramatic setting and characters (speakers) of the dialogue

Relationship with previous examples of the genre

Relationship with contemporary or near-contemporary works of any genre on the same topic(s)

Author versus persona: the relationship between the author and the narrator of the dialogue

Reading the work within and across: reading the dialogue on its own terms and also reading it in light of other dialogues or other works by the same author

---

2   Checklists or points to consider are very popular in introductory and intermediary literature on dialogues, particularly Platonic dialogues. The checklist assembled here attempts to include the most significant, commonly mentioned points.

CHAPTER I

EARLY GREEK DIALOGUE

The origins of dialogue are associated with Plato (424/423–348/347 BCE). Plato wrote when the genre was still in flux. The term *dialogos* is used in Plato's writings in two places, in *Laches* 200e and in *Republic* 1.354b but only to refer to a stretch of argument, not as a genre term.[1] It is possible that there were other types of dialogues before Plato and he was not the first one to write Socratic dialogues.[2] Plato is still a watershed figure for the genre, however, because he set the mold for the dialogues that came after. Consequently it is his dialogues that we will examine in this chapter. Below I will lay out the purpose, structure, and significant themes of the Platonic dialogues. I will show how the items in the checklist apply to the Platonic corpus as a whole before analyzing an individual dialogue, *Euthyphro*.

Plato was born in 424/423 BCE.[3] Diogenes Laertius, a third-century CE Greek author, records his genealogical details:

> Plato was the son of Ariston and Perictione or Petone, and a citizen of Athens; and his mother traced her family back to Solon; for Solon had a brother named Diopidas, who had a son named Critias, who was the

---

1   Andrew Ford, "The Beginnings of Dialogue: Socratic Discourses and Fourth-Century Prose," in *The End of Dialogue in Antiquity*, ed. Simon Goldhill (Cambridge: Cambridge University Press, 2008), 35.

2   Ibid., 29, 33. For pre-Socratic dialogues see Athenaeus, *The Learned Banqueters* (*Deipnosophists*) 11.505b–c; for other Socratic dialogues, see below.

3   For a more detailed chronological overview and discussion of Plato's family, see Debra Nails, "The Life of Plato of Athens," in *A Companion to Plato*, ed. Hugh H. Benson (Malden, MA: Blackwell, 2006), 1–12.

father of Calloeschrus, who was the father of that Critias who was one of the thirty tyrants, and also of Glaucon, who was the father of Charmides and Perictione. And she became the mother of Plato by her husband Ariston ... They say too that on his father's side, he was descended from Codrus, the son of Melanthus. (Diogenes Laertius, *Lives of the Eminent Philosophers* 3.1)[4]

Most of what we know about Plato's life comes from his own writings or from later sources such as that of Diogenes Laertius. His brothers fought in the Peloponnesian War (*Republic* 2.368a). Plato's kinsmen, Critias and Charmides, were part of the regime of the Thirty Tyrants in Athens; Plato himself was invited to join but declined (*Letter* 7.324d–325a). Plato was a student of Socrates and after his death (399 BCE), Plato moved to Megara (Diogenes Laertuis 2.106). When he began to write, we do not know. His philosophical ideas must have been circulating by 391 BCE as he was parodied in Aristophanes' *Assemblywomen* (see Introduction) which was produced in that year. 385 BCE marks the first of three trips to Sicily. Plato was invited to stay at the court of the Dionysius I, the tyrant of Syracuse. He was asked to serve as an advisor and an instructor in philosophy off and on for the Syracusan court, a task which he performed with little success and with increasing reluctance. His relationship with the ruling family at Syracuse would be a long-lasting one and a source of trouble and distress (*Letter* 7). Plato founded the Academy in the mid-380s. After escaping from Sicily one last time in 360 BCE, he renounced all further ties with that island and settled in Athens. He died there 348/347 BCE.

We are not certain of anything when it comes to Plato's reasons for writing and his reasons for choosing the dialogue form. There is some evidence to suggest that he chose this form in order to show what true philosophy entailed—a dialectical mode of examination

---

4   3.38 in Yonge. Translation taken from *The Lives and Opinions of Eminent Philosophers by Diogenes Laërtius*, trans. C. D. Yonge (London: George Bell & Sons, 1853).

and reflection—and to cause the reader to engage in a similar dialectical mode of thinking and reasoning.[5] To go back to the example
from the Introduction, when an ancient Greek read epic poetry he
understood that it would provide information about the world of
gods and heroes, that it would come in verse form, and that it would
use metaphorical language. He would come to it as an experienced
reader of myth and that would form his expectations as a reader. In
the case of the readers of Plato's dialogues, we are not sure what sort
of expectations the readers would have had as we do not know how
long the genre of dialogue had existed before Plato wrote, whether it had had time to develop conventions and how flexible these
might be.[6] There was never, even in antiquity, one agreed upon explanation for the origins of this genre.[7] It has also been suggested
that even philosophy itself was ill-defined at this time.[8]

Several of Socrates' associates wrote dialogues.[9] The extant remains
of these are in Xenophon, Plato, and in fragments of Aeschines.[10]

---

5   More on this below.

6   Ruby Blondell, *The Play of Character in Plato's Dialogues* (Cambridge:
     Cambridge University Press, 2002), 37 stresses the uniqueness of his dia-
     logues both in respect to predecessors and successors.

7   Simon Goldhill, "Introduction: Why Don't Christians Do Dialogue?"
     in *The End of Dialogue in Antiquity*, ed. Simon Goldhill (Cambridge:
     Cambridge University Press, 2008), 3.

8   Nightingale, *Genres in Dialogue*, 10, 14-15, argues that it was Plato whose
     work solidified the meaning of "philosophy" as a distinct enterprise.
     Before Plato the word was less defined and meant something like "intel-
     lectual cultivation." In Plato's writings, the Greek verb "to philosophize"
     comes to refer to "a distinct mode of living and thinking."

9   Ford, "Beginnings of Dialogue," 29, 33.

10   Nightingale, *Genres in Dialogue,* 4. Aeschines wrote several dialogues of
     which we have substantial fragments for two, *Aspasia* and *Alcibiades.* For
     a discussion of the fragments of Aeschines and bibliography, see Charles
     H. Kahn, "Aeschines or Socratic Eros," in *The Socratic Movement*, ed.
     Paul A. Vander Waerdt (Ithaca, NY: Cornell University Press, 1994), 87-
     106. At least six apologies were written for Socrates (Ford, "Beginnings
     of Dialogue," 32). See below for Xenophon's *Memoirs of Socrates*
     (*Memorabilia*); Xenophon's *Hiero* was a dialogue between Simonides,
     the poet, and Hiero, the tyrant of Syracuse (478–467 BCE) on how to

Sokratikoilogoi is the phrase Aristotle uses to describe these writings and he highlights the difficulty in classifying these, stating that "no common term" could be applied to them (*Poetics* 1447b).[11]

Ancient writers created theories about the nature of Plato's dialogues. It was stated before that there is some evidence to suggest that he chose this form in order to show what true philosophy entailed—a dialectical mode of examination and reflection—and to cause the reader to engage in a similar dialectical mode of thinking and reasoning. This is consistent with the description of the evolution of philosophy in antiquity as recorded by Diogenes Laertius who tells us that philosophy started out as the study of nature (*physikos*) or natural philosophy, to which Socrates added the study of ethics and Plato, bringing the field to perfection, dialetics (Diogenes Laertius 3.56).

Our surest means of determining why Plato used the dialogue form is not ancient testimony but rather internal evidence from the dialogues themselves. The dialogues share features in common in terms of their structure and message. These give us the clues we use to uncover Plato's purpose. The central figure of the dialogues is usually Socrates (or occasionally a wise "stranger," who serves much the same role). Socrates engages the other characters depicted in the dialogues in a series of questions and answers. No matter the ostensible starting point, eventually it is revealed that what is actually at stake is the definition of true goodness and the purpose of human life. When Socrates or the main speaker is engaging with others, he typically states premises which are then examined for consistency

---

be a good tyrant. *Economics* has as its main focus household management. Socrates and Critoboulus, the son of Crito, open the dialogue but the work includes a dialogue within a dialogue as Socrates recounts an earlier conversation he had with Ischomachus. Topics include wealth, agriculture, wives, slaves, and leadership. In the *Symposium*, Socrates and companions discuss a number of topics including love (a central topic in Plato's *Symposium*).

11   The translation is taken from *Aristotle's Theory of Poetry and Fine Art with a Critical Text and Translation of The Poetics*, trans. H. S. Butcher, 4th ed. (New York: Macmillan, 1920).

and truthfulness. This characteristic form of questioning is called the *elenchus*. Earlier philosophers had used a somewhat similar method.[12] By the time of Plato this word meant "examination of a person's words for truth and falsity" (see Herodotus 2.115) or the negative result of such an examination (*Gorgias* 473b).[13] In Plato it seems to be refutation or a test (see for example *Philebus* 52d). The term is also connected to the term "dialectic" in such a way as to suggest that it is an integral part of that process.[14] *Theaetetus* 161e describes Socrates' method of dialetics as the examination of the notions and opinions of others, and the attempt to refute them.[15] The purpose of this refutation and dialectical question and answer is to get to a proper understanding of ultimate realities.

---

12   Parmenides appears to have used this method. In Parmenides fr. 7 the idea is to consider alternatives and defend one's own ideas. Gorgias also did this, going through options and critiquing them one by one on which see James H. Lesher, "Parmenidean *Elenchos*," in *Does Socrates Have a Method? Rethinking the Elenchus in Plato's Dialogues and Beyond*, ed. G. A. Scott (University Park, PA: Penn State University Press, 2002), 34. For a discussion of other methods contained in Plato's dialogues see Hugh H. Benson, "Plato's Method of Dialectic," in *A Companion to Plato*, ed. Hugh H. Benson (Malden, MA: Blackwell, 2006), 98 and Michelle Carpenter and Ronald M. Polansky, "Variety of Socratic Elenchi," in *Does Socrates Have a Method? Rethinking the Elenchus in Plato's Dialogues and Beyond*, ed. G. A. Scott (University Park, PA: Penn State University Press, 2002), 89–100.

13   Charles M. Young, "The Socratic Elenchus," in *A Companion to Plato*, ed. Hugh H. Benson (Malden, MA: Blackwell, 2006), 56. The history of the term before Socrates is discussed in Lesher, "Parmenidean *Elenchos*," 19–35.

14   On dialetic see Blondell, *Play of Character*, 368 and Christopher Gill, "Afterword: Dialectic and the Dialogue Form in Late Plato," in *Form and Argument in Late Plato*, eds. Christopher Gill, and Mary Margaret McCabe (Oxford: Clarendon Press, 1996), 285. *Exetaxis* is another Greek term that Plato's Socrates will sometimes use to describe his method of examining people or ideas but it too, is linked to the term *elenchus* (see *Apology* 23c; 29e). On *exetaxis* see Harold Tarrant, "*Elenchos* and *Exetasis*: Capturing the Purpose of Socratic Interrogation," in *Does Socrates Have a Method? Rethinking the Elenchus in Plato's Dialogues and Beyond*, ed. G. A. Scott (University Park, PA: Penn State University Press, 2002), 61–77.

15   See also *Republic* 7.534b–c.

And when I speak of the other division of the intelligible, you will understand me to speak of that other sort of knowledge which reason herself attains by the power of dialectic, using the hypotheses not as first principles, but only as hypotheses—that is to say, as steps and points of departure into a world which is above hypotheses, in order that she may soar beyond them to the first principle of the whole; and clinging to this and then to that which depends on this, by successive steps she descends again without the aid of any sensible object, from ideas, through ideas, and in ideas she ends (*Republic* 6.511b–c).[16]

Only dialetic can bring us to reality (*Republic* 7.532e–533a). Dialetic belongs to the true philosopher (*Sophist* 253e).

Plato's dialogues, then, have an overarching consistency in form and content. Within this overarching consistency, there are significant variations. Blondell identifies two main presentations of Socrates in Plato's dialogues, the *aporetic*, or *elenctic*, and the constructive.[17] The *elenctic* Socrates is primarily a questioner: he interrogates his interlocutors (the persons who pose questions) and forces them to reexamine their preconceived notions; he claims to have no knowledge himself (for example, *Apology* 22d). In the dialogues in which he figures, the dialogue ends in *aporia* or in lack of closure. Old ideas are shown to be untenable but no new conclusions are reached. The constructive Socrates is more willing to acknowledge a position as his own; he is less open-ended and is willing to put forth concrete

---

16   Unless otherwise specified, all translations of Plato are taken from *The Dialogues of Plato*, trans. Benjamin Jowett, 3rd rev. ed., vol. 3 (Oxford University Press, 1892).

17   Blondell, *Play of Character*, 10–11. She names a third in the introduction but the bulk of her book deals with these two. The third is described in the following way: "One of these, whom I shall call 'Plato's Sokrates,' 'the Platonic Sokrates,' or just 'Sokrates,' is the maximal figure who emerges from the corpus as a whole, who maintains, at a bare minimum, the same identity and name, with all the ideas and traits that are ascribed to him" (10).

ideas; he is also more willing to discuss in full—and therefore to take seriously—ideas that he will ultimately discard.[18]

The addition of a constructive Socrates to the dialogues most likely indicates that Plato had concerns that the *elenchus* manner of dialectical engagement was not producing enough positive results. Socrates is most often presented as failing in the *aporetic* dialogues; he does not change people's minds.[19] This Socrates will demonstrate only that his partners in the dialogue have no more knowledge of the truth than he has. We might characterize this type of encounter as Plato attempting to show what philosophy was by showing what it was *not*.[20] The problem then was to generate positive content for philosophy and to explain how truth *was* to be obtained.[21] In the longer, constructive dialogues, such as *Republic* and *Laws*, positive concrete suggestions for living a life devoted to the good are provided. The Q and A format is still retained. What has changed in these dialogues is the participants. In order to receive Socrates' ideas one must have the right kind of character and intellectual capacity; only some people are fit by nature for right education (*Statesman* 309b).[22] Plato implies that it was the failure of the individual characters of the interlocutors in the *aporetic* dialogues rather than the method of Socrates that was at fault.[23] In the constructive dialogues

18   Blondell, *Play of Character*, 11. An example of this is the *Theaetetus'* long section on knowledge as perception which is discarded; on a willingness to acknowledge a position as his own see Gill, "Afterword," 290–292.

19   Blondell draws these conclusions from her analysis of the dialogues on the basis of themes and structures, 13, 125–127.

20   Nightingale, *Genres in Dialogue,* 11. The *elenchus* method does lead to the conclusion that some things are false. This is valuable in itself, see Rebecca Kamtekar, "Plato on Education and Art," in *Oxford Handbook of Plato*, ed. Gail Fine (Oxford: Oxford University Press, 2008), 343.

21   Hugh H. Benson, "Problems with the Socratic Method," in *Does Socrates Have a Method? Rethinking the Elenchus in Plato's Dialogues and Beyond*, ed. G. A. Scott (University Park, PA: Penn State University Press, 2002), 113.

22   Blondell, *Play of Character*, 125–127; Gill, "Afterword," 285.

23   Blondell, *Play of Character*, 187–188.

Socrates carefully chooses his interlocutor; he pre-selects to get better results and as a consequence is able to make more progress.[24]

Why does Plato choose to write about philosophy in this form? A strong possibility is that the dialogue form is used in order to draw the reader into the discussion as a participant. When the questions appear in the text, the reader is forced to consider them. When no definitive answer is provided in the text, the reader then has to supply one for him/herself. Another function of the forum is to avoid any hint of dogmatism. Being encouraged to draw one's own conclusions is the polar opposite of the dogmatic approach and we can see that later generations in antiquity thought that Plato's dialogues were non-dogmatic (Cicero, *On Academic Scepticism* 1.16). It is easy to see how this interpretation fits the *aporetic* dialogues. But this is true also of the constructive dialogues. Socrates' character is, of course, the most privileged. Even in dialogues in which other views are discussed at length, his views receive the most favorable treatment.[25] But through having his Socrates constantly stressing the need to reexamine and to question, Plato purposely draws attention to the lack of an authoritative voice.[26] We can contrast this approach with other philosophers of the day who did present their teachings as deity-inspired, in the manner of poet or a prophet.[27] Plato's Socrates inverts the traditional teaching hierarchy: in his view, he himself is a student rather than a teacher.[28] The dialogue form consequently provides a model for how to approach the philosophical life: it shows us how to engage in a life of examination and a never-ending search for truth and goodness.

---

24   Gill, "Afterword," 289.

25   Blondell, *Play of Character*, 40–43.

26   Gill, "Afterword," 283–311; Michael Frede, "Plato's Arguments and the Dialogue Form," in *Methods of Interpreting Plato and his Dialogues*, eds. James C. Klagge, and Nicholas D. Smith (Oxford: Clarendon Press, 1992), 214, 215; Frede, "The Literary Form of the Sophist," in *Form and Argument in Late Plato*, eds. Christopher Gill, and Mary Margaret McCabe (Oxford: Clarendon Press, 1996), 136–137 and 139–142.

27   Blondell, *Play of Character*, 39.

28   Ibid., 77–79.

Now that we have explored the general aim of Plato's dialogues, it is time to turn to the checklist and consider how this information informs the way we use these dialogues to do history.

Audience: Plato's works were published and circulated in his lifetime so at a minimum he must have wanted to reach the reading public. We can see from Old Comedy that philosophical ideas were to an extent "in the air" which may possibly suggest that the intended audience is then not necessarily only the literate but everyone.[29] Those who can actually become true philosophers, however, Plato certainly believed to be an elite group.

Frame: The frame is the setting in which the dialogue takes place. The frame for the dialogues includes the location, time, and the characters that are present as the dialogue proceeds. All of these details may impact the way the dialogue is to be read.

As an example, the *Symposium*'s setting is Athens, the year before the Sicilian Expedition. The opening of this dialogue, 172a–174a, devotes considerable space to establishing when and where the original dialogue took place, and how the record of that dialogue has been passed down to the present day. The attention devoted to explaining the long chain through which this conversation has passed highlights how far removed is the original event from the present. The narrator is Apollodorus, a follower of Socrates. As the *Symposium* opens, he is speaking to his intimate friends and promising to recount to them, in response to their request, the dialogue that took place between Socrates and company some 16 years before. He explains that he had just recounted the episode recently (the day before yesterday) to one Glaucon who had also asked to hear it. In the original dialogue event there were several people present and events which took place before that occasion are also narrated. The chronological layers and chain of transmission are as follows:

Socrates' talks with Diotimia, a Mantinean prophetess
(201d–212a);

Alcibiades has previous encounters with Socrates
(217a–221c)

The original dialogue event takes place (174a-223d)

Phoenix and Apollodorus hear about the dialogue
from Aristodemus who was present; Apollodorus also
hears about the dialogue from Socrates (173b)

The dialogue is recounted to Glaucon by someone
who heard it from Phoenix (172b)

Apollodorus recounts the dialogue to Glaucon
(173b–c)

Apollodorus recounts the dialogue to his intimate
friends (172a; 173c; 174a-223d)

The reader reads the dialogue as recounted by
Apollodorus

as crafted by Plato

Plato has multiple tiers to play with here. The framing invites the readers to view the arguments from within the frame and without.[30] He can manipulate the relationship of the original event with the narrator Apollodorus and his circle, and the relationship between each of these layers (original event and the event of the recounting) to the reader. One way that he does this is through characterization.[31] Each of these layers (distant past, dialogue event, and present day) has its own set of characters, some of whom are historical (like Alcibiades) and some of whom are clearly wholly created (like Diomitia, the prophetic woman from Mantinea with whom Socrates conducts a dialogue-within-the-dialogue). Even the

---

30 Mary Margaret McCabe, "Form and the Platonic Dialogues," in *A Companion to Plato*, ed. Hugh H. Benson (Malden, MA: Blackwell, 2006), 51.

31 This is Blondell's approach.

narrator, Apollodorus, who appears but briefly, is given a characterization. He is described as one who is "crazy" (*to manikos*) for philosophy (173d).

What should we, as the readers, do with this information? The individual characters may work in several ways. One thing that seems to always be true is that the character of individuals in dialogues is directly related to their real lives.[32] Aristotle describes this type of thinking in *Rhetoric* 1356a when he states "The proofs provided through the instrumentality of the speech are of three kinds, consisting either in the moral character of the speaker or in the production of a certain disposition in the audience or in the speech itself by means of real or apparent demonstration."[33] Aristotle is writing about oratory here but the idea was commonplace in antiquity. The dialogues take place in the past; by the time the reader engages with the text, he knows whether what is said—the whole outlook or orientation of the character—has been vindicated or not.[34] In the *Symposium*, Alcibiades bursts suddenly into the midst of the dinner party, drunk and rowdy. He describes his relationship with Socrates and praises him profusely (212d–222b). But this speech is taking place only a year before he would be implicated in the scandal of the parody of the Mysteries and the defamation of the Herms, a turning point in his relationship with Athens to which city state he would prove to be no true friend. We must question then whether we are to take his portrayal of Socrates as accurate. This is particularly true since Alcibiades himself tells us that Socrates' words have layers and that one must look beyond the surface (221e). Is Plato using this character to present a false view of Socrates that he wishes the reader to reject?

Allusions to the true life histories of a dialogue's participants are not the only way that Plato characterizes them. Names of dialogue characters can be generic, or particular, or both, as in the case of Hippias

---

32   McCabe, "Form and the Platonic Dialogues," 47.

33   Translation taken from *The Rhetoric of Aristotle*, trans. J. E. C. Welldon (New York: Macmillan, 1886).

34   Blondell, *Play of Character*, 32–34, 113.

who stands for a typical sophist but retains individual character-istics within the dialogue.[35] And Blondell warns that while Plato must logically use the fact that his readers would know some of the most public facets of his characters' lives (such as the infamous Alcibiades) that does not mean that Plato intended to *always* con-vey characters that meshed with *all* of the known historical facts.[36]

Taking together everything that has been noted about Plato and his dialogues up to this point, we can see that these dialogues of Plato are literary creations. This was known also in antiquity.[37] We know that Plato has an agenda (to encourage a philosophical life). He tells us, through his use of frames and distancing techniques (there are at a minimum three levels: Socrates and his interlocutors; Plato's relationship with Socrates; and Plato's relationship with us) that he is not intending to record for us real historical events.[38] Even when, consequently, he includes historical figures in his dialogues, we can-not use the dialogues to learn about these historical persons—we must instead use the historical persons to interpret the dialogues.[39] For the historical Socrates, for example, sources include Plato's di-alogues, Greek comedies, Xenophon's dialogues, and Aristotle. Plato's depiction of Socrates does not fully correspond with any of these sources and the personality and teaching style of his Socrates is inconsistent across the dialogues. Of course, we would not nec-essarily classify Plato's dialogues as a *worse* source for the historical Socrates than these others (Aristophanes is certainly not interested in drawing us an accurate portrait) but the point is that despite his

---

35 Blondell, *Play of Character*, 68–69.

36 Ibid., 35-36.

37 Athenaeus, *The Learned Banqueters* 11.505d–506a; see also 11.505b; on Timon of Phlius and his criticism of Socrates writing fake conversa-tion (frr. 19; 62) see A. A. Long, "Plato and Hellenistic Philosophy," in *A Companion to Plato*, ed. Hugh H. Benson (Malden, MA: Blackwell, 2006), 428.

38 Rosemary Desjardins, "Why Dialogues? Plato's Serious Play," in *Platonic Writings/Platonic Readings*, ed. Charles L. Griswold (University Park, PA: Pennsylvania State University Press, 1988), 112, 123–125.

39 As exemplified in Blondell.

many works that include Socrates as a main character, Plato is still not a strong source for the historical Socrates' beliefs and actions.[40] We must exercise a similar caution when using Plato as a source for the other characters (such as Alcibiades).

Author versus persona: We must not assume that the dominant speaker in the dialogue always represents Plato's own voice.[41] The main speaker is usually Socrates. But sometimes it is someone else (as for example in *Laws*, *Sophist*, and *Statesman*). If the dialogue is giving more airtime to one set of views over another, then we might assume that Plato agrees with that view (else why prioritize it?) but we do have to pause to consider. The construction of the *aporetic* dialogues at least suggests that they are not intended to present the last word on any subject.

Reading within and across: Each dialogue must be approached in two ways: it must be read as a complete work in itself (taken on its own terms as it were) but must also be read in light of other works (particularly other dialogues) by that same author.[42] For Plato, we can identify overarching constants across all of the dialogues. Plato's dialogues assume that we can know the good through philosophy and dialectic (the examination of previously held and often faulty beliefs).[43] Some dialogues clearly indicate that they are in fact to be

---

40   William J. Prior, "The Socratic Problem," in *A Companion to Plato*, ed. Hugh H. Benson (Malden, MA: Blackwell, 2006), 25–35. Plato is specifically mentioned as not being present on the day of Socrates's death (*Phaedo* 59b).

41   Blondell, *Play of Character*, 17–21.

42   Blondell, *Play of Character*, 10. Individual context is determinative for Carpenter and Polansky, "Variety of Socratic Elenchi," 89–100; Christopher Gill, "Dialectic and the Dialogue Form," in *New Perspectives on Plato, Modern and Ancient*, eds. Julia Annas, and Christopher J. Rowe (Cambridge, MA: Harvard University Press, 2002), 152–161 suggests that our primary task should be to read each dialogue on its own terms (rather than in light of other dialogues); Christopher J. Rowe, *Plato and the Art of Philosophical Writing* (Cambridge/New York: Cambridge University Press, 2007), 1–51 suggests that Plato tries to progressively educate the reader across the dialogues.

43   Rowe, *Plato*, 25–28 and 273–276.

read in light of others as they explicitly refer to each other (see for example the opening lines of the *Statesman*).[44]

There are also repeating themes in the dialogues. Here is a quick list of some of the more prominent: citizenship, consistency between word and deed, poetry and the visual arts, political life, philosophy, the limitations of language, education, knowledge, false experts, sophists, rhetors, imitation, law, religion, laughter, drama (comedy and tragedy), the nature of reality, sense perception, and the nature of the soul. Many of these feed into each other as for example in the case of knowledge, experts, and education. Plato frequently addresses how we obtain true knowledge and of what it consists.[45] This is in turn related to the educational system: how we can learn and how we pass things on to others (*Laws* 6.765d–e).[46] Plato's Socrates bemoans the lack of experts everywhere and individual dialogues attack different types of traditional experts: poets, natural philosophers, sophists, and rhetors.[47] A running theme throughout Plato's dialogues is that these traditional authorities cannot teach virtue and need to be replaced with dialectic.[48]

It will be helpful to look briefly at some of these themes since they will help us understand Plato better and because many of them recur in the dialogues of later generations. As we proceed through this select survey, we will note in passing the writings of contemporaries or near-contemporaries who wrote on similar topics (in accordance with our checklist: Relationship with contemporary or near-contemporary works of any genre on the same topic(s)). We will give

---

44 Blondell, *Play of Character*, 314.

45 See below for references.

46 On education and teaching in Plato and his time, see Kamtekar, "Plato," 336–359.

47 These will be discussed below. In addition to these, Socrates critiques the "eristic" or disputatious style (*Euthydemus* 277d–278d).

48 Alternatively, we might understand Socrates as one who does not want to abandon the past but to re-interpret received tradition. Plato himself may be taking this approach toward the teaching of Socrates; see Desjardins, "Why Dialogues?," 122–124.

particular attention to the theme of religious belief and practice as this topic is of central concern to two of the sample dialogues which we will analyze in this study.

Sophists are the subject of several Platonic dialogues. By the 450s BCE, sophists were educators for hire who prepared men for political careers.[49] Sophists were foreigners and as such were mistrusted (Plato, *Protagoras* 313b; 316c–d; compare Isocrates, *Exchange of Properties* (*Antidosis*) 155–156).[50] They took money for their services which fed into the negative stereotype present in the dialogues (*Protagoras* 310d; 311b–314b; *Sophist* 223a–b; 225e–226a; 231d; and *Theaetetus* 161d–e; *Meno* 91b–d).[51] Sophists in Plato's view charm their listeners with eloquence so that they are not inclined to critically examine but instead become merely passive recipients (*Protagoras* 315a–b).[52] Just as important is the fact that sophists do not know that of which they speak.[53] They only imitate reality (*Sophist* 234a–235b; 268b–d) and, being deceptive imitators, they are only capable of corrupting (*Meno* 91b–d).[54]

Rhetors, or public speakers, are characterized very similarly. In *Gorgias* Socrates all but concludes that rhetors and sophists are in

---

49 T. H. Irwin, "Plato: The Intellectual Background," in *The Cambridge Companion to Plato*, ed. Richard Kraut, (Cambridge: Cambridge University Press, 1992), 63-68.

50 Nightingale, *Genres in Dialogue,* 22–25.

51 Some scholars do not think that Socrates has a wholly negative view of sophists. It is true that Socrates does not seem to be categorically denouncing the teaching of Protagoras. In *Meno*, he defends him as being a good sophist in 91d–e. But good sophists are the exception rather than the rule in the dialogues. And in *Protagoras*, the sophist is still challenged on the grounds that his views, while not necessarily incorrect, are still unexamined.

52 Blondell, *Play of Character*, 97.

53 In *Protagoras* sophists are those who sell doctrines for the soul. This is a dangerous practice as they do not know what they are selling (313d–314b; see also *Meno* 91b–d; 95c–96b; *Sophist* 233b–c).

54 *Republic*, Book 3; *Euthydemus* and *Greater Hippias* also critique sophists. Imitation will be discussed further below.

fact one (465c). Both practices consist of a form of flattery whose only aim is to gratify the audience (463a–b). Rhetoric can only offer pleasure to the audience; it is incapable of contributing to personal betterment (like poetry, 502b–503b). In *Euthydemus*, skill in speechmaking is likened to the sorcerer's art in its ability to charm (289d–290a). Rhetors, like sophists, do not know that of which they speak (*Gorgias* 465a).[55]

Natural philosophers who explained the workings of the world through natural laws and principles were also a target for Plato (see for example *Laws* 10.886d–890d). Plato views them as instigators of atheism (*Laws* 10.886d–e and 10.890a).[56] Like other self-proclaimed authorities, they do not have true knowledge of their subject matter (of being and nonbeing; *Sophist* 242c–252d).

Poets perhaps come in for the most stringent and sustained criticism of all the established authorities. According to *Republic* 10.607b, the quarrel between poetry and philosophy is an old one. This may or may not be true (Plato may be exaggerating), but in Plato's dialogues there is no question that the two forms of learning, poetry and philosophy, are enemies.[57] Plato wanted to banish or regulate poetry because poets claim to be giving truth when they are really not.[58] The poets (Homer and Hesiod are mentioned often) have incorrect ideas about the gods (*Euthyphro* 5e–6c, *Republic* 2.364c–e, and *Laws* 10.886c).[59] They cannot be trusted to compose proper

---

55 In *Ion* rhapsodes are even further removed from reality and the ability to convey goodness than poets as they recite the words of poets—they do not know the things the poets describe (537a–542b).

56 Irwin, "Plato: The Intellectual Background," 79: some of them believed in a divine creator but some did not; see 51–58 for survey of passages of natural philosophy in Irwin.

57 Nightingale, *Genres in Dialogue,* 60 argues that this was a piece of rhetoric.

58 Christopher Janaway, "Plato and the Arts," in *A Companion to Plato,* ed. Hugh H. Benson (Malden, MA: Blackwell, 2006), 392.

59 Blondell, *Play of Character,* 381 n. 277; Xenophanes the sixth-century founder of the Eleatic School reproached poets for attributing shameful things to the gods (Diogenes Laertius 9.18); Heraclitus the philosopher (c. 535–c. 475 BCE) considered them to be unreliable (Diogenes

prayers and are not able to discern the good; in an ideal state, they would be regulated by the authorities (*Laws* 7.801a–d and *Republic* 3.401b).[60]

Poets, as we might expect, are therefore depicted as another group who do not have true knowledge of what they depict (*Apology* 22c). Poets give merely a reflection of their own souls rather than a faithful reproduction of the truth or the real.[61] Since poets are incapable of reflecting the truth, poetry cannot educate or help people. Poets (like rhetors) try to please the audience rather than to better them. To do this, they appeal to the bad part of the human soul, the emotional part. Poets try to cultivate and stimulate the emotional and their attention is on the worst parts of the human character.[62] What they have to offer is imitation and bad imitation at that (*Republic* 3.392a–398b; 10.598a–608b). It was believed that poetry or the emotional performance of a story would enchant the listener or reader and endow him with mimetic impulses.[63]

Imitation (*mimesis*) is a key concept in Plato.[64] The foundational idea behind much of Plato's critique of poets, sophists, and rhetors

Laertius 9.1); discussed in Elizabeth Asmis, "Plato on Poetic Creativity," in *The Cambridge Companion to Plato*, ed. Richard Kraut, (Cambridge: Cambridge University Press, 1992), 340.

60 There are some indications that perhaps he was not wholly adverse to every kind of poetry; in *Republic* 10.607a hymns and praises to gods are acceptable forms of poetry; see also Asmis, "Plato on Poetic Creativity," 344–346.

61 Ibid., 352–353.

62 Asmis, "Plato on Poetic Creativity," 354–356.

63 Blondell, *Play of Character*, 96–97. In *Hippias Minor*, which may or may not have been written by Plato, Socrates lays out the problems he had with poetry and sophists, two interconnected ways of educating (128). Hippias is representing the use of Homer as an educational tool and the interpretation of Homer and the kind of thinking that supports and welcomes this type of education in other works (136). Plato's Socrates is not consistently against Homeric heroes; he depicts Achilles and Odysseus as positive models on occasion (158). Even in *Hippias Minor* he upholds some aspects of these characters (160).

64 For more on the concept of imitation in Plato see Amasis and Blondell.

is that imitation could influence character development.[65] The role of imitation in education and the shaping of one's character is evident in the works of Plato' contemporary Isocrates (436–338 BCE) who tells us that praiseworthy speeches or discourses should use only the most fit and useful examples which will influence the speaker not only in his discourse but in his very life (Isocrates, *Exchange of Properties* 277). Compare this with the description of the guardians in *Republic*:

> [O]ur guardians, setting aside every other business, are to dedicate themselves wholly to the maintenance of freedom in the State ... they ought not to practice or imitate anything else; if they imitate at all, they should imitate from youth upward only those characters which are suitable to their profession—the courageous, temperate, holy, free, and the like; but they should not depict or be skilful [*sic*] at imitating any kind of illiberality or baseness, lest from imitation they should come to be what they imitate. Did you never observe how imitations, beginning in early youth and continuing far into life, at length grow into habits and become a second nature, affecting body, voice, and mind? (*Republic* 3.395b–d)

Ancient Greeks thought that not only real persons could shape character but also that representations of good and bad examples in any media could do so. In the stories of the poets (epic, tragedy, and comedy) there was a relationship between the character conveying the ideas and the impact of those ideas (see for example *Republic* 3.392a–398b; 6.500c; 10.598a–608b; and *Laws* 7.816e).[66] The consumer (audience/reader) was thought to assume the character's point of view, feelings, etc. and so to imitate them.[67] An emotional identification with the speaker was dangerous (see especially Book

---

65   Janaway, "Plato and the Arts," 390–391.

66   Blondell, *Play of Character*, 80.

67   Ibid., 81.

10 of the *Republic*; Aristotle *Poetics* 1462a and *Politics* 1336b).[68] In the classical idea of mimetic pedagogy, the characters of stage or literature were supposed to reinforce what is already in one (whether good or bad). The problem with viewing bad characters, consequently, was that they would reinforce one's latent badness. Ancient audiences were supposed to reject negative characters in plays, for example, precisely because they were not supposed to feel affinity with them.[69] In Book 3 of *Republic*, the underlying idea is that in imitating the good one becomes the self one is meant to be by developing the latent goodness within; this is the only proper type of imitation.[70] In post-Platonic dialogues, as we will see, there is a move away from this very narrow classification of profitable models.

Poetry is related to the theme of sense perception as is the discussion of other types of art. Although ideally all the arts would provide examples of goodness, visual art like poetry is but an image of true reality (and therefore deceptive; *Republic* 3.401c; 10.596e).[71] Sense perception and its relationship with reality is a recurring topic in the dialogues (*Phaedo* 65a–66a; 74d–76a; 83a–c; cp. 99e; *Republic* 6.511b–c; 7.523a–c; *Sophist* 235d–236c; 260c; 266e; and *Theaetetus* 151e–164b).[72]

As in his examination of the arts and the senses, so in his examination of language, Plato questions how and if language is capable of conveying reality. Whereas poets and sophists use language to persuade, "Plato sought to change language into an instrument of investigation and moral reform."[73] In *Phaedrus* 275c–276a, Socrates disparages the written word which, when questioned, always says

---

68   Ibid., 90; Janaway, "Plato and the Arts," 392–396.

69   Blondell, *Play of Character*, 88–93.

70   Blondell, *Play of Character*, 238.

71   Asmis, "Plato on Poetic Creativity," 349; on the visual arts see Janaway.

72   Covered in Deborah K. W. Modrak, "Plato: A Theory of Perception or a Nod to Sensation?," in *A Companion to Plato*, ed. Hugh H. Benson (Malden, MA: Blackwell, 2006), 366–367.

73   Asmis, "Plato on Poetic Creativity," 341.

the same thing (Plato, *Phaedrus* 275d).[74] The written word is but the image of the spoken word (276a). But spoken language too can also be but a deceptive image as we have already seen.

> And may there not be supposed to bean imitative art
> of reasoning? Is it not possible to enchant the hearts of
> young men by words poured through their ears, when
> they are still at a distance from the truth of facts, by
> exhibiting to them fictitious arguments, and making
> them think that they are true, and that the speaker is
> the wisest of men in all things? (*Sophist* 234c).[75]

Another theme that recurs in Platonic and later dialogues is that of the conflict between a life of active political engagement and the life of the detached philosopher.[76] The *Republic* for instance gives us the constitution for an ideal society, the *Laws* a more pragmatic, scaled-back version.[77] Nightingale in her book points out that we can understand Plato's position best by placing him in contradistinction to his contemporary, Isocrates. Isocrates had his own ideas about what a philosopher should be. He did not think that philosophers were, or should be, outsiders. In his view, they should work within the Athenian social and political fabric (see *Exchange of Properties* 60–61 and 205–206). Plato thought that philosophers should take up issues that impinge upon or shape the social and political life of society: because philosophy in his view dealt with ultimate realties, the insights of philosophy would theoretically impact everything all the time. But unlike Isocrates, he thought that the philosophers were inevitably always outsiders. We can see this best in the allegory

---

74   Plato says he has not written any philosophy (*Letter* 7.341c–e); writing is not where one puts one's serious thoughts (344c–d); (books cannot do Q and A (*Protagoras* 329a). See Desjardins, "Why Dialogues?", 111 for discussion of this topic.

75   Jowett translation, vol. 4.

76   Blondell, *Play of Character*, 298–303.

77   Trevor J. Saunders, "Plato's Later Political Thought," in *The Cambridge Companion to Plato*, ed. Richard Kraut, (Cambridge: Cambridge University Press, 1992), 483.

of the cave: the philosopher, as one of the few who truly knows the Good, stands apart from his fellow man. Having visited the divine, he must return to earth and help to lead the blind to the light. But he will be mocked and perhaps even killed (*Republic* 7.517a).[78]

The last theme from the Platonic dialogues that we will examine is religion. The goal of philosophical inquiry is to know the Ultimate Realties and the best way to live. The connection to religion is therefore obvious and philosophers regularly discussed the nature of the gods and humanity's tie to them. We have seen already that the dialogues express criticism of false depictions of the gods as found among the natural philosophers and the poets. Plato thought that producing virtue and wisdom by improving our souls is to give the best type of service to the gods (*Apology* 29d–30b).[79] But Plato did not think that everyone was capable of the highest form of service. A true philosopher's existence is not possible for the multitude (*Republic* 6.494a).[80] In an ideal state, the bulk of humanity would render service to the gods via a well-regulated polis cult (on state regulation see *Laws* 6.759a–760a; 7.799a–b; 7.803e–804b; Book 10). There were some things that he wanted to change about traditional religion: in his ideal state there would be restrictions on private cult and on the terms of priesthoods (*Laws* 4.717b; 6.759d; 10.909d–910d); he disapproved of joking in religious ceremonies, of the emotional impact of hymns, and of course of poetic depictions of the gods.[81] But his views on state cult were conventional

---

78   See discussion in Nightingale, *Genres in Dialogue,* 26–59.

79   Mark L. McPherran, "Platonic Religion," in *A Companion to Plato*, ed. Hugh H. Benson (Malden, MA: Blackwell, 2006), 246; Jon D. Mikalson, *Greek Popular Religion in Greek Philosophy* (Oxford: Oxford University Press, 2010), 29 argues that "service to the gods" is the closest we get to a definition of religion in Greek thought and we see this in Plato.

80   *Laws* presents a two-tiered theology, one for the philosophically ready/ competent and one for everyone else (through polis cult) on which see Michael L. Morgan, "Plato and Greek Religion," in *The Cambridge Companion to Plato*, ed. Richard Kraut, (Cambridge: Cambridge University Press, 1992), 241–244.

81   For myths and joking see Mikalson, *Greek Popular Religion*, 60–66; for hymns *Laws* 7.800d–e.

in many respects: the gods exist and they are good (*Laws*, Book 10); the *Timaeus* describes a divine craftsman (see also *Statesman* 271d–275c, God as a shepherd); he endorsed all the usual types of veneration (prayer, sacrifices, and hymns) to the Olympians, the state gods, underworld gods, *daimones*, heroes, and ancestral deities (*Laws* 4.716d; 4.717a–b; 7.801d; 7.803e–804b; 7.799a). In his ideal society, the city authorities would determine religious practices but he also envisioned consulting the Oracle of Apollo. This too, was conventional, cultic regulation being a regular function of the Delphic Oracle (see *Republic* 4.427b–c; *Laws* 6.759c–d).

> What, then, he said, is still remaining to us of the work of legislation? Nothing to us, I replied; but to Apollo, the God of Delphi, there remains the ordering of the greatest and noblest and chiefest things of all. Which are they? he said. The institution of temples and sacrifices, and the entire service of gods, demigods, and heroes; also the ordering of the repositories of the dead, and the rites which have to be observed by him who would propitiate the inhabitants of the world below. These are matters of which we are ignorant ourselves, and as founders of a city we should be unwise in trusting them to any interpreter but our ancestral deity. He is the god who sits in the centre, on the navel of the earth, and he is the interpreter of religion to all mankind. (*Republic* 4.427b–c)

Many philosophers wrote about divination.[82] We can see in the writings of the Roman Cicero (who would himself write a dialogue on this subject) that their views were well known.

> But some exquisite arguments of philosophers have been collected to prove why divination may well be a true science. Now of these philosophers, to go back to the most ancient ones, Xenophanes the Colophonian appears to have been the only one who admitted the

---

82   Mikalson, *Greek Popular Religion*, 110–129.

existence of Gods, and yet utterly denied the efficacy of divination. But every other philosopher except Epicurus, who talks so childishly about the nature of the Gods, has sanctioned a belief in divination; though they have not all spoken in the same manner ... (Cicero, *On Divination* 1.5).[83]

Plato in *Phaedrus* prefers the ecstatic kind of divination (that is, deity-inspired) as opposed to a divination that was practiced through learned techniques.[84] In *Symposium* 202e–203a, *daimones* or spiritual beings bridge the gap between moral and immortal worlds. Socrates' own *daimon* is mentioned at *Apology* 31d and 40a; *Euthydemus* 272e; *Phaedrus* 242b–c; *Theaetetus* 151a; and *Republic* 6.496c. To have a *daimon* was also not uncommon. There was a name for such people—or for their *daimones*—"belly talkers." The name arose from the idea that the *daimon* was speaking from within the person.[85] Johnston points out that Greeks and Romans wrote about divination more than on any other type of religious practice.[86] This makes sense because messages from the beyond were open to interpretation and could be easily manipulated. Plato grouped soothsayers with those who dealt in the despicable chicanery of spells and charms:

> And mendicant priests and soothsayers [*manteis*] go to rich men's doors and persuade them that they have a power committed to them by the gods of making an atonement for a man's own or his ancestor's sins by sacrifices or charms, with rejoicings and feasts; and they promise to harm an enemy, whether just or unjust, at

---

83   In Yonge's numbering, *On Divination* 3. All translations of this text are taken from *The Treatises of M. T. Cicero: On the Nature of the Gods; On Divination; On Fate; On the Republic; On the Laws; and On Standing for the Consulship*, trans. C. D. Yonge (London: George Bell & Sons, 1878).

84   Sarah Iles Johnston, *Ancient Greek Divination* (Malden, MA: Wiley-Blackwell, 2008), 8.

85   See for example in Aristophanes, *Wasps* 1019–20; Johnston, *Ancient Greek Divination*, 140.

86   Johnston, *Ancient Greek Divination*, 4.

a small cost; with magic arts and incantations bind-
ing heaven, as they say, to execute their will. (*Republic*
2.364b–c)[87]

In *Meno* 99c, diviners and soothsayers speak under the power of divine inspiration but they do not themselves know what they are saying; that is, diviners can say true things but not of their own accord.
Plato believed that some divination could be real but false diviners
were included in his critique of false experts.[88]

We have been looking here at themes that persist across the dialogues. But as was noted above, there are reasons to read each dialogue on its own without relevance to how the same theme appears
in other works. The fact that there are issues with consistency across
the dialogues would seem to support this. David Sedley compares

---

87 I have altered the translation of the first line very slightly; see also *Laws*
10.909b which is very similar.

88 Mikalson, *Greek Popular Religion*, 126 on Plato and types of diviners;
on diviners and types of diviners in general, see Johnston, *Ancient Greek
Divination*, 109–143 and Michael Flower, *The Seer in Ancient Greece*
(Berkeley: University of California Press, 2008), 22–71. Flower does not
think that Plato's views on divination were normative. The following are
singled out: the categorization of divination into artificial and natural
types (85–87, 241); the conflation of seers (*manteis*) with begging priests
(*agurtai*) and wizards (*magoi*), (see especially 28–29, 65, 69–70); the depiction of the *daimones* in *Symposium* 202e–3a as intermediaries in the
process of divination (89); according to Flower, Plato is the only classical
author to state that all humans have a prophetic part of the soul (which is
located in the liver) (7-8); in Plato's view, only the divinely inspired female
prophetesses (the Pythia, the Sibyl, the priestesses at Dodona) were truly
valid (84-86). Of these, the idea that Plato was the first to divide divination into natural and artificial types is plausible though not certain. It does
mesh with Plato's prevalent theme of false experts. Flower writes, "Plato
is determined to represent the practitioners of nonecstatic divination as
the practitioners of mere *technē*, and a faulty one at that, and this is part
of his attempt to devalue the importance of technical divination in Greek
society" (85). But it must be noted that although Plato may have been
attempting to impose a rigid, two-tiered, categorization onto a sphere of
activity which was much more fluid in reality, he still includes artificial
or technical divination in his ideal society, as Flower notes himself (*Laws*
8.828b and 9.871d; Flower, 139 n. 9).

Plato's differing explanations of knowledge across the dialogues.[89]
Republic and *Timaeus* discuss knowledge with reference to the
Theory of Forms but *Theaetetus* does not reference the Forms; in
Republic and *Timaeus,* knowledge (*epistēme*) and opinion (*doxa*)
are different but in *Theaetetus* knowledge is a type of opinion; in
Meno, Phaedo, and *Phaedrus,* knowledge is recollection but this
is not mentioned in the *Theaetetus* and in this work the mind in
infancy is empty. Diogenes Laertius complains about the obscurity of Plato's dialogues and suggests method for dealing with this
complexity:

> And the explanation of his arguments is threefold. For
> first of all, it is necessary to explain what each thing
> that is said is; secondly, on what account it is said,
> whether because of its bearing on the principal point,
> or figuratively, and whether it is said for the purpose
> of establishing an opinion of his own, or of refuting
> the arguments brought forward by the other party to
> the conversation; and thirdly, whether it has been said
> truly (Diogenes Laertius, *Lives of Eminent Philosophers*
> 3.65)[90]

In short, we must be open to the possibility that there is not one set
message about any given theme. It is better to see the dialogues as
intentionally providing layers of meaning or having competing messages which must be allowed to co-exist.[91] Such intentional complexity was not unusual in the antiquity and is reflected in Greek,
Roman, and early Christian writings.[92]

---

89 On knowledge across the dialogues (he is comparing *Theaetetus* to oth-
    er dialogues) see David Sedley, "Three Platonist Interpretations of the
    Theaetetus," in *Form and Argument in Late Plato,* eds. Christopher Gill,
    and Mary Margaret McCabe (Oxford: Clarendon Press, 1996), 84–85.

90 3.38 in Yonge.

91 Kenneth M. Sayre, *Plato's Literary Garden: How to Read a Platonic
    Dialogue* (Notre Dame, IN: University of Notre Dame Press, 1995), 201;
    Rowe, "Plato," vii; Desjardins, "Why Dialogues?," 113.

92 Pythagoras for example had two levels of instruction—see Diogenes

Now we turn to the analysis of a specific dialogue, *Euthyphro*, so that we might see the checklist in action, drawing out any fruitful implications in regard to audience, frame, relationship with previous examples of the genre, author versus persona, reading within and across, and in light of contemporary or near-contemporary authors.

Euthyphro

The dialogue opens in the portico of the king archon's court (2a). The king archon was in charge of trials for impiety in ancient Athens and Socrates reveals to Euthyphro that he has been indicted.[93] The frame here suggests an apologetic intent: if Socrates' trial is referenced, his unjust execution is also brought to mind. And indeed we will see this theme carried throughout the dialogue. The characterization that Socrates makes of Meletus, his indictor, is telling:

> What is the charge? Well, a very serious charge, which shows a good deal of character in the young man, and for which he is certainly not to be despised. He says he knows how the youth are corrupted and who are their corruptors. I fancy that he must be a wise man, and seeing that I am the reverse of a wise man, he has found me out, and is going to accuse me of corrupting his young friends. And of this our mother the state is to be the judge (2c).[94]

There is heavy sarcasm here: "he *says* he knows ..." he *must* be a wise man." Even if we had no other dialogues to which to compare this one we would be suspicious of these words of Socrates. But read in light of other dialogues, in which the theme of *thinking that one knows*

Laertius 8.15; Cicero tells us that Heraclitus deliberately adopted obscurity (*On Ends* 2.15); Christians would develop allegorical scriptural interpretation and the Gnostic communities in particular were heavily invested in the idea that a text could be constructed so as to have different meanings for different readers).

93 Aristotle, *Constitution of the Athenians* 57.2.

94 Jowett translation, vol. 2.

that which one does not know is ubiquitous, we can already guess that Meletus is an unreflective person who has brought a charge about piety without truly understanding what piety is.

In this and in the section following, we learn of Socrates' indictment, who brought it, and Meletus' motivation. Meletus claims that he brings the charge on behalf of the traditional gods whom Socrates has injured (3b).

Euthyphro in his response tells us several things:

1) Meletus will bring an accusation against Socrates for having a divine helper or "sign"

2) and for making innovations in religion

The charge of innovation in religion meshes with accounts of the trial found in other sources (Xenophon, *Memoirs of Socrates* (*Memorabilia*) 1.1.1; *Apology* 11; Plato, *Apology* 24b–c; Diogenes Laertius 2.40). His *daimon*, as we have seen, was mentioned at *Apology* 31d and 40a; *Euthydemus* 272e; *Phaedrus* 242b–c; *Theaetetus* 151a; and *Republic* 6.496c.

Then he gives us new information about himself and Athenian society:

3) The people of Athens are very ready to heed slanders about religious innovations (3b)

4) Euthyphro himself has a reputation for being abnormally religious: he frequently stands up in the assemblies and foretells the future which earns him the ridicule of his peers (3b–c)

This framing of the dialogue gives us grist for the characterizations of Euthyphro and it tells us something about Athenian political–religious life. The indication here is that "god-talk" is a not-uncommon feature of Athenian political debate but also that it was not always taken seriously. Socrates' indictment shows us that it certainly could be a serious matter for the state but Euthyphro's negative reception in the assembly tells us that it was not *automatically* accorded serious consideration. Further we will consider whether there may be an apologetic tinge to this message. For now, we can see that Euthyphro has revealed himself to be a religious enthusiast, pronouncing his divine communications *ad nauseum*. As Euthyphro ascribes the negative reaction of the assembly to jealousy we can infer that he thinks highly of himself. When he adds that he will not be put off by rejection but will instead force his peers to pay attention, we are obviously to infer that he is an obnoxious person (3c). A comparison naturally presents itself to the mind of the reader: Socrates was an irritating personality who claimed a special connection with the divine. As readers we wonder: will Euthyphro operate as a foil for Socrates? When we find next that he is to see the king archon so that he may indict someone, we automatically also compare him to Meletus. Is Euthyphro going to be another person who brings charges against an elder though he is himself inexperienced and ignorant?

When Socrates hears that Euthyphro is bringing a charge against his father for murder, we see his irony once again: "By the powers, Euthyphro! How little does the common herd know of the nature of right and truth. A man must be an extraordinary man, and have made great strides in wisdom, before he could have seen his way to bring such an action" (4a–b). The language here echoes that used to describe Meletus. It also, through the phrase, "how little does the common herd know" raises the issue of the difficulty of discerning the good that we see in so many Platonic dialogues.

When Euthyphro explains in more detail what his father had done and his reaction to it, the language used is reminiscent of many Socratic dialogues and of the *elentic* Socrates. Euthyphro says that a slave of his own had attacked and killed a house slave and that his father had bound the man up and cast him into a ditch while he went to consult the religious authorities about the proper measures to take next. The man meanwhile died. His death, Euthyphro says, was technically a murder and as such resulted in a religious pollution equal to that of the first murder. The style of his reasoning reminds us of Socrates:

> I am amused, Socrates, at your making a distinction between one who is a relation and one who is not a relation; for surely the pollution is the same in either case, if you knowingly associate with the murderer when you ought to clear yourself and him by proceeding against him. The real question is whether the murdered man has been justly slain. If justly, then your duty is to let the matter alone; but if unjustly, then even if the murderer lives under the same roof with you and eats at the same table, proceed against him (4b–c).

He speaks as one who wants to get at the ultimate truth, to not allow particulars to obscure the reality or the first principles. There is one thing that causes pollution and one remedy for cleaning it. We cannot help but think: would not Socrates say the same?

Euthyphro, like Socrates, has his objectors: his family members object that the father's neglect did not amount to murder and that even if it did, it is actually impious to prosecute one's father. They object that he has incorrectly defined murder and that he has not considered that there is another rule of piety to consider. Euthyphro's response though is reminiscent of Socrates for he questions their right knowledge of piety. "Which shows, Socrates, how little they know what the gods think about piety and impiety" (4e).

Now we are certain that Euthyphro, though superficially like Socrates, is in reality a faux-Socrates. He is indeed that worst of all types: the man who thinks he knows but does not. Socrates now questions him: are you not afraid that you will get it wrong? His reply betrays an overweening self-righteousness: "The best of Euthyphro, and that which distinguishes him, Socrates, from other men, is his exact knowledge of all such matters. What should I be good for without it?" (5a). Euthyphro is clearly standing in for the unreflective Socratic interlocutor.

There follows more ironic questioning from Socrates who characterizes Euthyphro as a false expert. He states his intention to become Euthyphro's pupil and invites him to explain what are piety and impiety; holiness and unholiness (5c–d). In the reminder of their exchange, Socrates continues to challenge Euthyphro for a correct definition of piety, a test which the young man fails.

Included in this section is the idea that holiness is a part of justice (12 c–d). We can compare here *Laws* 10.887b in which the gods establish justice and *Protagoras* 331a–332a, which also discusses the relationship between justice and holiness, or *Phaedo* 75c–d, which lists the examination of the just and the holy among the proper concerns of philosophical inquiry. This was a concept very familiar to Greek readers.[95] The Greeks believed that Zeus had given justice to men (Hesiod, *Works and Days* 274–285) and Euthyphro begins his defense by pointing to Zeus as a precedent. Zeus himself, the father of justice, bound his father Cronus as punishment when he devoured his own children (6a), therefore, he, Euthyphro is justified in indicting his own father for murder.

Socrates challenges this reliance on the poetic tradition (6a–c). We have seen how this theme runs throughout the Platonic dialogues. It was not an idea which originated with Plato. Poetic conceptions of the gods had already been criticized in the works of Xenophanes and Heraclitus and the comic playwrights regularly mocked anthropomorphized deities in the theater. Xenophanes the sixth-century founder of the Eleatic School reproached poets for attributing shameful things to the gods (Diogenes Laertius 9.18); Heraclitus the philosopher (c. 535–c. 475 BCE) considered them to be unreliable (Diogenes Laertius 9.1). In Old Comedy, the human characteristics of the gods provided the foundation for many jokes and comical scenes involving deities. Situations which contained potential for comedy for human characters: love affairs, bodily functions, the passions (greed, gluttony, lust, and anger); over-indulgence of any

---

95 Mikalson, *Greek Popular Religion*, 204–206 thinks that on the contrary Plato represents an exception here in his belief that the Greek deities were concerned about human justice.

kind—these were also the situations in which anthropomorphized gods could be depicted. Eupolis (c. 446–c. 411 BCE) for instance was said to have created a famished Heracles, timid Dionysus, and adulterous Zeus (see Σ Aristophanes *Peace* 741b).[96]

As we have seen previously, the idea that humans should render service to the gods in the form of prayer and sacrifice (13b–15a) was a commonly held notion in ancient Greece. We do see this in the writings of other near-contemporaries. In the fragments of Aristotle's successor, Theophrastus, to sacrifice is to honor the gods and a man who is close to the gods must be one who sacrifices constantly.[97]

The focus of Socrates' cross-examination is not these conventional notions of piety (which elsewhere Plato endorses, *Laws* 7.799a; 7.803d–804b; Book 10) but rather Euthyphro's unreflective, arrogant assumption that he knows what piety is and is living according to it. After driving him into an exposure of his ignorance, Socrates finally delivers his *coup de grâce*: surely you must know or else you would not be so ready to prosecute your father in the name of piety! (15d).

There is very likely an apologetic function to this dialogue. Early in the dialogue, Socrates complains that Euthyphro is allowed to self-designate as a close companion of the deity without penalty. "For I observe that no one appears to notice you—not even this Meletus; but his sharp eyes have found me out at once, and he has indicted me for impiety" (5c). He ends by alluding again to his indictment for religious innovation and his failed hope that

---

96   Bernard Freydberg, *Philosophy & Comedy: Aristophanes, Logos, and Erōs* (Indiana: Indiana University Press, 2008), 42 notes that these same issues (justice, the authority of the poetic tradition) are comically rendered in Aristophanes, *Clouds* 901–906 in which there is a debate about justice between Just Cause and Unjust Cause. In the play, Unjust Cause asks how justice can be said to exist, given the fact that Zeus, who bound his own father, went unpunished? Given the high degree of similarity between the two works, it is likely that the playwright was intending to evoke Platonic teaching in this scene.

97   William W. Fortenbaugh, *Theophrastean Studies* (Stuttgart: Franze Steiner Verlag, 2003), 183, 187.

Euthyphro might have shown him a way to elude it by allowing Socrates to demonstrate what true holiness was (15e–16a). The implication here is surely that the Athenians who condemned Socrates to death did not know what true piety was (Xenophon stresses in his Socratic works the conventional piety of Socrates, see in particular his dialogue, *Memoirs of Socrates* 1.1.1; 4.8.11; *Apology* 5; 11; 19).

Let's return to the checklist and summarize our results.

Audience: The audience would be the same as for any Platonic dialogue.

Relationship with previous examples of the genre: Plato is the starting point for us for dialogues but we can see that the apologetic function (Socrates was a pious person, unfairly targeted) is evident in the dialogues of Plato's contemporary, Xenophon. Xenophon's *Memoirs of Socrates* contains numerous short exchanges between Socrates and challengers or friends (and one between Alcibiades and Pericles). These were overtly apologetic, serving to explain his teachings and establish him as a good man.

> Such was Socrates; so helpful under all circumstances and in every way that no observer, gifted with ordinary sensibility, could fail to appreciate the fact, that to be with Socrates, and to spend long time in his society (no matter where or what the circumstances), was indeed a priceless gain. Even the recollection of him, when he was no longer present, was felt as no small benefit by those who had grown accustomed to be with him, and who accepted him. Nor indeed was he less helpful to his acquaintance in his lighter than in his graver moods (Xenophon, *Memoirs of Socrates* 4.1.1).[98]

Frame: The characterization of Euthyphro is key to understanding the message of the dialogue. It is connected also to the apologetic function of the dialogue.

---

98 Translation taken from *The Works of Xenophon*, trans. H. G. Dakyns, vol. 3.1 (New York: Macmillan, 1897); see also 4.8.11.

Reading within and across: Several themes reappear in this dialogue including Socrates as the unjustly accused, the problematic nature of divination, the problematic nature of poetic depictions of the gods, and the relationship between piety and justice.

Reading in light of contemporary works on similar topics: In this dialogue, Plato's Socrates, despite the accusations against him, is depicted as being one who fits into pre-existing categories of Greek religious experience (his *daimon*) and reflects commonly held beliefs about the gods and the best way to honor them (the gods love justice; humans render service to the gods through just living, sacrifices, and prayers) which we see reflected in other works of approximately the same time period, including the works of pre-Socratic and post-Plato philosophers.

Author versus persona: The persona in this dialogue is Socrates. Given the apologetic message and the correspondence between the ideas expressed by Socrates in this dialogue and other Platonic dialogues it is unlikely that there is a great distance between the view of Plato himself and the views expressed by Socrates.

CHAPTER II

ROMAN DIALOGUE

The Romans inherited the dialogue genre from the Greeks. M. Iunius Brutus the Elder was the first to compose dialogues in Latin. He used the form to write about Roman civil law (Cicero, *On the Orator* 2.223–224). According to a list made by the early church father, Jerome, Varro wrote several works (which he termed *logistorici*) which seem to have included dialogues. None of these works has survived. Cicero (lived 116–27 BCE) embraced the form for his philosophical writings and writings about oratory. After Cicero, there is no other extant Latin dialogue until Tacitus' *Dialogue on Oratory*. This chapter will survey Cicero briefly and then present an analysis of Tacitus' *Dialogue on Oratory*.

Cicero's philosophical dialogues were part of his self-imposed project of delineating an educational model for the Roman statesman, which would include philosophy and oratory (fields he saw as related). Cicero had studied philosophy in Rome, Athens, and Rhodes (*Brutus* 315–316) and he admired Plato and Aristotle.[1] Cicero seems to have accepted, at least in theory, Plato's conviction that Socratic dialetic was necessary to get to the truth. He styled himself an adherent of the Academic school which he traced back to Socrates:

> But, as it is the peculiar property of the Academy to interpose no personal judgement of its own, but to

---

1   "[A]fter having given us a treatise on the Commonwealth, it appears a natural consequence that you should also write one on the Laws. For this is what I see was done by your illustrious favorite Plato, the philosopher whom you admire and prefer to all others, and love with an especial affection" (Cicero, *Laws* 1.15; Yonge translation; 1.5 in Yonge's numbering). Cicero modeled some of his works after Plato (*Republic*, *Laws*) and he translated Plato's *Protagoras* and *Timaeus*.

admit those opinions which appear most probable, to
compare arguments, and to set forth all that may be
reasonably stated in favour of each proposition; and so,
without putting forth any authority of its own, to leave
the judgement of the hearers free and unprejudiced; we
will retain this custom, which has been handed down
from Socrates; and this method, dear brother Quintus,
if you please, we will adopt as often as possible in all our
dialogues together (*On Divination* 2.150).[2]

His dialogues, accordingly, do sometimes exhibit the quick dialectical Q and A of Plato's *aporetic* Socrates. But Cicero also wrote longer, sustained discourses which he patterned after Aristotle. In the Aristotelian model of philosophical inquiry, interlocutors ask questions briefly and are answered at length.[3] Cicero himself was not an

---

2   Yonge translation; numbered in Yonge as *On Divination* 72; see also
     Cicero, *Tusculan Disputations* 1.8; *On Ends* 2.1–3. Elsewhere criticisms of
     the dialectical method are expressed reminiscent of the concerns of Plato
     (as presented in Blondell). In *On the Nature of the Gods* 1.11, the dialetic of Socrates is described as being a negative type that offers no positive
     content; compare criticism of dialetic as expressed by dialogue participant
     M. Antonius in *On the Orator* 2.157. In *Laws* 1.62, Cicero advocates for
     the full, continuous style as a means of effective discussion in contrast to
     the Socratic style dialetic: "And all these acquirements he will secure and
     guard as by a sort of fence, by the knowledge how to distinguish truth from
     falsehood, and by a certain science and art of reasoning which teaches him
     to know what consequences follow from premises, and what proposition
     is contrary to another. And when such a person feels that nature has designed him for civil society, he will not rest contented with these subtle
     disquisitions alone, but will put in practice that more comprehensive and
     continuous eloquence by which he may be able to govern nations, to establish laws, to punish malefactors, to defend the honest part of mankind,
     and publish the praises of great men: by which also he may fitly put forth
     precepts of safety, and panegyrics of virtue, in a way suited to persuade
     his countrymen: by which also he may be able to rouse them to the practice of virtue, and turn them from wickedness, to comfort the afflicted,
     and, in fine, to immortalize the wise consultations and noble actions of
     the brave and wise, and to punish the shame and infamy of wicked men
     by handing them down in undying records" (Yonge trans.; 1.24 in Yonge's
     numbering).

3   See for example *Tusculan Disputations* 1.17; 2.9; *On Fate* 1–4; on the

adherent of any one school (although he did claim to be) and he was less interested in presenting accurate histories of philosophical schools than in laying out alternative philosophical positions for his readers.[4] For *On Academic Scepticism* Cicero provides an example of how the speeches were composed and why he chose the characters he did:[5]

> I have therefore composed a dialogue purposing to be held between us in my villa at Cumae, Pomponius being there also. I have assigned to you the doctrines of Antiochus, which I thought I understood to have your approval; I have taken those of Philo for myself. I imagine that when you read it you will be surprised at our holding a conversation, which we never did hold; but you know the usual method of dialogues (Cicero, *Letters to Friends* 9.8).[6]

---

mixed Platonic and Aristotelian structures of the dialogues, see Malcolm Schofield, "Ciceronian Dialogue," in *The End of Dialogue in Antiquity*, ed. Simon Goldhill (Cambridge: Cambridge University Press, 2008), 67–70. Schofield suggests that Cicero's later dialogues (composed 45, 44 BCE) are more open-ended than Plato's—that is, that Cicero presents alternative points of view more fully and with less judgment, leaving it up to the reader to decide which has the better argument (62–63); Cicero claims to do this in *On Divination* 2.150.

4 For examples of Cicero's philosophical adherence, see *On Academic Scepticism* 1.13; *On the Nature of the Gods* 1.10–12; *On Duties* 2.7–8; *Tusculan Disputations* 2.5; on the motivations behind Cicero's presentation of the various philosophical schools, see Carlos Lévy, "Cicero and the New Academy," in *The Cambridge History of Philosophy in Late Antiquity*, ed. Loyd P. Garson (Cambridge: Cambridge University Press, 2010), 2.2/ Kindle loc. 1714–1756.

5 On the frames for Cicero's dialogues, see J. G. F. Powell, "Dialogues and Treatises," in *A Companion to Latin Literature*, ed. Stephen Harrison (Oxford: Blackwell, 2005), 232–233.

6 Translation taken from *The Letters of Cicero*, trans. Evelyn S. Shuckburgh, vol. 3 (London: George Bell and Sons, 1900) where the numbering is given as 9.6. In *On the Orator* 2.9, he notes some are alive who knew the men depicted in the dialogue so that he cannot wholly fabricate; in 3.16 Cicero tells us that he received his information about Crassus and Antonius from Cotta and that he thinks he is doing a good job (!) of representing the style

Even though Cicero's dialogue participants present the best case for each side, and even though he sometimes makes a pretense of objectivity or inscrutability, Cicero is quite willingly to give his own views.[7] He was also not above eliding the differences between philosophical schools to create the impression of a general harmony between them that meshed with the message he wished to support.[8]

In Cicero we see some of same themes as in the Platonic dialogues. Cicero would present views of the philosophical schools on issues such as religion (as for example in his trilogy *On the Nature of the Gods, On Divination, On Fate*; also *Laws*, Book 2) and sense perception (and its relation to reality).[9] He was overtly apologetic fairly often, responding with vigor to the denigration of philosophy which was common among his Roman contemporaries (*On Academic Scepticism* 2.4–7; *Tusculan Disputations* 2.4; *On Ends* 1.1–3) and in defense of particular schools (*On Academic Scepticism*). He wanted to show that the Latin language, and by extension, elite Roman authors such as himself, were up to the challenge of handling discourse on serious subjects (*On Ends* 1.1, 4–11); he wanted to show that he was using his leisure time (unfairly thrust upon him) in the service of the state, to improve his fellow Romans through introducing

---

of both men; see also *On Friendship* 3–5.

7   These often come at the beginning or end of works; see for example, the end of *On the Nature of the Gods* 3.95.

8   See for example, *Tusculan Disputations* 4.6; *On Academic Scepticism* 1.43; and *On the Nature of the Gods* 1.11–12. On Cicero's views in the dialogues see Schofield, "Ciceronian Dialogue," 78–81 and Powell, "Dialogues and Treatises," 232– 233; on suppressing differences and creating false harmony see Lévy, "Cicero and the New Academy," 3.2/Kindle loc. 1948–1957.

9   *Phaedrus* was a model for Cicero and passages from this dialogue were worked into Cicero, see Powell, "Dialogues and Treatises," 233. *Phaedo* inspired *Tusculan Disputations*, Book 1 on the soul and immorality (Paul MacKendrick, with the collaboration of Karen Lee Singh, *The Philosophical Books of Cicero* (New York: St. Martin's Press, 1989), 7). On religious laws for the ideal state see *Laws* 2.19–22; on sense perception see *On the Nature of the Gods* 1.12; *On Academic Scepticism* 1.19–55 and 79–91; *On Ends* 1.64; 2.36–37; *On the Orator* 3.25–26; on virtue and the happy life see *Tusculan Disputations*, Book 5; *Laws* 1.60; *On Old Age* 77.

them to the usefulness and value of philosophical teaching (*On Academic Scepticism* 2.6; *On Ends* 1.10; *On the Nature of the Gods* 1.7); he wanted to show that Roman culture was superior to Greek culture.[10] The education of the orator is another topic that Cicero engages with at length.[11] This theme will be taken up by Tacitus.

Cicero's outlook differed from Plato in that he was less interested in uncovering ultimate realties than he was in putting philosophical doctrines to practical use.[12] Cicero was a proponent of the philosophical statesman. In Cicero's view, education (which included philosophy, poetry, and oratorical training) should be used in the service of the state. The *Republic*, for instance, begins with a defense of the active political life as opposed to a life of leisure. Whereas the philosopher cannot persuade people to do good, the statesman can compel obedience (1.3). Wise men must not suffer the wicked to rule the state (1.9).

Oratory, which Plato condemned as imitative and deceptive, Cicero saw as being compatible with the practical, philosophical statesman.[13]

> For the orator has a great affinity to this system of philosophy which we follow; for he borrows subtlety from the Academy, and in return he imparts to it a certain richness of expression, and copiousness of ornament (*On Fate* 3).[14]

---

10   On which see Schofield, "Ciceronian Dialogue," 77–78.

11   This occurs in *On the Orator* especially; see for example 1.20–21; 3.54–55, 86–90; *Orator* 113–122.

12   In *On the Nature of the Gods* 1.7 Cicero says that all the doctrines of the philosophers have a practical bearing and that he himself has put them into use in both his public and private life.

13   *On the Orator* includes a critique of Plato's division between oratory and thinking or tongue and brain (3.60–73); in *Orator* 11–16 Cicero criticizes the Platonic rejection of oratory and argues that the marriage of philosophy and oratory is necessary.

14   Yonge translation; Yonge numbering is *On Fate* 2.

Contra Plato, Cicero believed that it was a good thing that the orator could sway the emotions. From a pragmatic perspective, emotions, not judgment, are often the deciding factor for the audience (*On the Orator* 2.178).[15] In fact oratory is said to be not only compatible with philosophy but superior to it in that an orator can sway people to the right course (2.35; see also 1.75). Whereas in Plato's conception, philosophy is for the select few, Cicero's contention is that philosophy should be presented so that it is accessible for all educated persons (*Tusculan Disputations* 2.8). Oratory in the Roman system must be for the multitude (*On the Orator* 2.159). Similarly, Cicero's primary interest in poetry is in how it may most effectively be used as a tool of persuasive speaking.[16]

In the same way that Cicero engages with the themes raised in Plato's dialogues, but presents his own unique views, so Tacitus will engage with the themes raised by Cicero in his own *Dialogue on Oratory*. It is by reading Tacitus' dialogue in light of the earlier work of Cicero that we can appreciate its full meaning. Tacitus in effect uses his dialogue to become part of the ongoing conversation about education, oratory, and the responsibilities of the Roman elite man in the Roman state. We will see him engage with Cicero and with Plato as well as with other contemporary or near-contemporary literature that addressed the use and techniques of oratory.[17] But

---

15   See also 1.17, 53, 60, 222–223; 2.205–215; the speaker must himself feel the emotions so as to effectively convey and to incite emotion in the audience as well as to empathize with his client 2.189–192; praise for the practical, Roman orator is included in 1.32, 260.

16   Cicero's dialogues do sometimes comment in passing on the truth-value of poetry but he is more interested in the practical aspect of how use it in persuasive speaking. He also thinks that poetry can be used in moral instruction. In *Tusculan Disputations* 2.27 poets are harmful because they portray strong men behaving weakly and so engender unmanliness. Plato was right to ban them from his ideal state. Yet as the dialogue continues, the poets are utilized for a positive example, a Roman version of Greek play in which a strong man behaving weakly overcomes his effeminacy by use of reason (2.48–50).

17   J. Allison, "Tacitus' *Dialogus* and Plato's *Symposium*," *Hermes* 127 (1999): 479–492.

scholars differ over which parts of the received tradition, that is, which themes, Tacitus most wishes to engage with and this results in different interpretations of the dialogue and Tacitus' purpose in writing it. In what follows the dialogue will be analyzed according to three different versions of our checklist, each generated from a recent reading of the dialogue.

Dialogue on Oratory

Tacitus (c. 56–after 117 CE) was a Roman provincial of the equestrian class. His political career included posts as suffect consul and proconsul of Asia. He was a skilled orator, delivering at least two speeches of some renown. The first was a funeral speech for Lucius Verginius Rufus, the governor of Germania Superior, who had defeated Vindex; the second was a prosecution speech against the proconsul of Africa, Marius Priscus, for corruption. In addition to his dialogue, Tacitus left us two histories of Rome, *Annals* and *Histories*; a biography of his father-in-law, *Agricola*; and *Germania*, a description of the German tribes.

His writing style is elegant and his narrative engaging. He is also a central source for information about the Julio-Claudian emperors and the Year of the Four Emperors following the assassination of Nero. These factors ensure the Tacitean corpus a privileged status. But Tacitus wrote in an enigmatic style. We are never sure how cynical he actually was about the Roman government or how far we should trust him. The *Dialogue on Oratory* contributes to our assessment of Tacitus' perspective on the *principate* (that is, rule by Roman emperors, Augustus to Carus) and his agenda as an author.

The dialogue opens with the narrator, ostensibly Tacitus himself, addressing one Justus Fabius. Fabius has asked the narrator to explain the decline of oratory. The narrator in reply recounts an event from his youth in which learned men took up this very theme. The dialogue, then, purports to be a recounted event, a literary device already made common by Tacitus' predecessors in the genre. The dialogue proper consists of two series of paired speeches followed by a final speech by Maternus. The characters are Aper, Secundus, Messala, and Maternus. The first scene of the dialogue opens after Maternus has delivered a reading of his tragedy, *Cato*. In the first set of speeches, Aper presents arguments for engagement in public life, specifically the role of an orator and Maternus defends a life of retirement dedicated to literature, specifically the life of a poet. In the second set of speeches, Aper defends the superiority of modern orators to those of earlier generations and he is answered by Messala who argues for the superiority of the ancients and decries the decline in oratorical education. There is a break in the text and the last speech picks up mid-stream with Maternus who addresses the relationship between the political condition of states and the excellence of oratory. The dialogue ends with the speakers parting amicably.

Reading One: An Anti-imperial Reading

In this interpretation of the dialogue, Andrew Gallia argues that power and eloquence are the central motifs in the work. The message of the dialogue is that these two things invariably go together and are a dangerous combination.[18] Tacitus is against the imperial system, specifically against the imperial informants who denounce citizens before the emperor (the Latin form of the word is *delatores*), but he is not anti-emperor. He does not want to see a return to the Republic; he accepts the present political system of rule by one and he believes that the system can be run beneficially under a strong, capable ruler.

In this understanding of the dialogue, the audience would be Tacitus' contemporaries who were capable of picking up on the allusions he made to life in the Empire. They would have some knowledge of Republican history so as to be able to appreciate the references made to that time period. They would be able to identify allusions to Ciceronian dialogues. These contemporary, historical, and literary allusions would inform their reading of the work.

---

18   Andrew Gallia, "*Potentes* and *Potentia* in Tacitus's *Dialogus de oratoribus*," *Transactions of the American Philological Association* 139 (2009):169–206.

For Gallia, Maternus is the central character of the dialogue and his situation and his speeches should shape the way we interpret this work. Maternus is the host (3.1), he sets the topic of the ensuing discussion (4), moderates it (16.3 and 27), and delivers the final speech (36–41). The setting of the dialogue revolves around Maternus. The discussion takes place on the day after his play, *Cato*, has been performed and the reception of this work has led to a turning point in his life.[19] Maternus' play has offended powerful people (Gallia translates the passage in question as "offended the sensibilities of the powerful")[20] and this same adjective, the powerful (*potens* or *potentia*), is used later in the work to describe the informants (*delatores*).[21] These were men who made a name for themselves by denouncing and prosecuting others.[22]

Key to Gallia's interpretation is the idea that the characters who speak in the dialogue were all real people, recognizable to the readers of Tacitus' day.[23] And the people they mention in their conversation and speeches were also historical persons who would likewise be known to the readers. This is similar to the approach that Blondell advocates for interpreting the Platonic dialogues: the real lives of the figures mentioned in the dialogue provide clues to the message of the dialogue. For Gallia, the informants, Vatinius, Eprius Marcellus, and Vibius Crispus, described in Tacitus' dialogue as powerful persons and known to be in real life powerful persons, are used to show the link between oratory and personal power and to show the dangerous ways that oratory can be misused.[24]

---

19 Gallia, "*Potentes* and *Potentia*," 169; the evidence for Maternus as the central character is provided in n. 1

20 Ibid., 170.

21 Ibid., 172.

22 Ibid., 180. For evidence that the *delatores* were universally hated see Steven H. Rutledge, *Imperial Inquisitions: Prosecutors and Informants from Tiberius to Domitian* (London: Routledge, 2001), 11–15.

23 Gallia, "*Potentes* and *Potentia*," 170, n. 3 gives the historical evidence.

24 Ibid., 177; the sources for these men are discussed in Rutledge, *Imperial Inquisitions*; for Vibius Crispus see 278–282; for Eprius Marcellus see 225–228.

Cripsus and Marcellus had a bad reputation as prosecutors. They are described in 8.3, "[T]hey have now for many years been the most powerful men in the state."[25] Both men had survived Nero and were active at the time of the historical frame (Vespasian's reign).[26] They were able to rise through the imperial system solely through their oratorical abilities, as Aper tells us in his speech (8.3).[27] That Maternus' recent work, *Cato*, was aimed at the *delatores* is supported by his earlier tragedy through which, Maternus tells us (11.2), he was able to break the "wicked power" of another famous *delatores*, Vatinius. In his other works, Tacitus describes Vatinius as a squanderer (Tacitus, *Histories* 1.37) and the most powerful among the *delatores*: "After a time he grew so powerful by accusing all the best men, that in influence, wealth, and ability to injure, he was pre-eminent even in that bad company" (Tacitus, *Annals* 15.34).[28]

Gallia sees the connection between power and oratory carry over through all of the speeches. Whereas Aper praised the *delatores*, Maternus finds them to be morally corrupt (their eloquence is described as "money-getting and blood-stained" 12.2) and as having a false power.[29]

> As for your Crispus and Marcellus, whom you hold up to me as examples, what is there in their lot to be coveted? Is it that they are in fear themselves, or are a fear to others? Is it that, while every day something is asked from them, those to whom they grant it feel indignant? Is it that, bound as they are by the chain of flattery, they

---

25 All translations of this text are taken from *The Agricola and Germany of Tacitus and the Dialogue on Oratory*, trans. Alfred John Church, and William Jackson Brodribb, rev. ed. (New York: Macmillan, 1899).

26 Gallia, "*Potentes* and *Potentia*," 177; for the date, see 177–178 n. 23.

27 Ibid., 178.

28 This translation is taken from *Annals of Tacitus*, trans. Alfred John Church, and William Jackson Brodribb (London: Macmillan, 1882). The sources for Vatinius are in Rutledge, *Imperial Inquisitions*, 276, 277. Gallia discusses Vatinius and the *Cato* of Maternus, 190–192.

29 Gallia, "*Potentes* and *Potentia*," 180–183.

are never thought servile enough by those who rule, or free enough by us? What is their power at its highest? Why, the freedmen [by which he means imperial freedmen] usually have as much (13.4; Brodribb)[30]

The message of this dialogue is only uncovered via comparison with a predecessor. Maternus in his final speech refers to one of Cicero's dialogues on oratory, *Brutus*, and he overturns Cicero's theory of the relationship between civic order and eloquence expressed in that work. Maternus points to the political crises of the Republic to show that in that era, too, power and eloquence went hand in hand—and this was a bad thing at that time as well. "In both eras, the pursuit of power represents a dangerous ambition that leave one vulnerable to attack."[31]

Maternus states:

> [I]n the disorder and licence of the past more seemed to be within the reach of the speaker, when, amid a universal confusion that needed one guiding hand, he exactly adapted his wisdom to the bewildered people's capacity of conviction. Hence, laws without end and consequent popularity; hence, speeches of magistrates who, I may say, passed nights on the Rostra; hence, prosecutions of influential citizens brought to trial, and feuds transmitted to whole families; hence, factions among the nobles, and incessant strife between the senate and the people. In each case the state was torn asunder (36.2–4).

To Maternus, the flourishing of oratory is associated with civil disorder. In an ideal state (41.3–4) it would not be needed.[32] Cicero had described the relationship between the state and oratory in different terms; for him, the well-ordered state was a boon to oratory:

---

30 Ibid., 183.

31 Gallia, "*Potentes* and *Potentia*," 185.

32 Ibid., 185–186.

[F]or an emulation to shine in the forum is not usually found among a people who are either employed in
settling the form of their government, or engaged in
war, or struggling with difficulties, or subjected to the
arbitrary power of kings. Eloquence is the attendant of
peace, the companion of ease and prosperity, and the
tender offspring of a free and well-established constitution (*Brutus* 45).[33]

In Tacitus' dialogue, Maternus purposely recalls and rejects the
words of Cicero in *Brutus* when he says:

I am not speaking of a quiet and peaceful accomplish-
ment, which delights in what is virtuous and well regulated. No; the great and famous eloquence of old is the
nursling of the licence which fools called freedom; it is
the companion of sedition, the stimulant of an unruly
people, a stranger to obedience and subjection, a defi-
ant, reckless, presumptuous thing which does not show
itself in a well-governed state (40.2).

It is by comparing the dialogue to Tacitus' other works and works
by contemporaries that we can see that this denunciation of the
"bad powerful" is aimed not at the emperor but at the *delotores*. The
evidence is philological: the Latin word used in the dialogue to de-
note power, *potentia*, is not associated with the emperor in Tacitus
and the same is true of other contemporary authors.[34] Similarly, an
examination of the word *libertas* or freedom throughout Tacitus'
works supports this interpretation.

The difference between Maternus's position in the
Dialogus and Cicero's in the *Brutus* lies in their conception of what constitutes a "well-established state"
(*bene constituta civitas*) and the balance between per-

---

33   All translations of this text are taken from *Cicero on Oratory and Orators*,
     trans. J. S. Watson (New York: Harper & Brothers, 1875); the numbering
     for Watson is *Brutus* 12.

34   Gallia, "*Potentes* and *Potentia*," 173–174.

sonal freedom and stability that is attained therein. Maternus feels that abusive *licentia* fosters eloquence and suggests that a misplaced reverence for oratory causes the ignorant to mistake this quality for true *libertas*.[35]

Gallia points out that this term, *libertas*, was fluid and that true freedom was not incompatible, in the discourse of the imperial age, with the monarchy. Both Augustus and Vespasian claimed to restore "liberty" to the people. An anti-tyrant message is not the same as an anti-*princeps* message.[36] Maternus consequently is railing against the system of personal power and oratory rather than against the *princeps*.

Reading Two: An Intertextual Reading

In this second, intertextual, reading by Christopher van den Berg,[37] Tacitus is considered to be taking part in an ongoing conversation about oratory. Van den Berg finds numerous allusions to Late Republican and contemporary authors which suggest that Tacitus' primary focus is literary and intellectual: he, like his peers and literary predecessors, is keenly interested in what makes a good orator and in how the practice of oratory is evaluated. His motivation in writing is to demonstrate that the orators of his own day, of which group he himself was also a member, were no less talented than those of an earlier age.

The audience in this case must be those who had read the pre-existing and contemporary literature on what makes for effective oratory. The ideal reader must be one who could recognize the allusions to these works and be able to appreciate how Tacitus was distinguishing his own perspective in relation to them.

---

35   Ibid., 187.

36   Gallia, "*Potentes* and *Potentia*," 196–197.

37   Christopher S. van den Berg, *The World of Tacitus'* Dialogus de Oratoribus: *Aesthetics and Empire in Ancient Rome* (Cambridge: Cambridge University Press, 2014).

For Van den Berg, as for Gallia, the opening sets the theme and tone of the piece. This is what we should expect; the frame should signal to the reader the scope and function of the work. What Van den Berg finds striking is the fact that in the opening, the narrator does *not* say that there are no talented orators in the present only that they are not *called* this.[38] The narrator then immediately presents two contemporary orators, Aper and Secundus, who are described as being unfairly underrated, and he defends their learning and abilities in order to demonstrate that there are, in fact, quite superior, successful orators in the present era.[39] The recurring theme is thereby established, the "complex dynamic between renown and *eloquentia*," that is, how rhetoric has been and is currently being evaluated.[40] Throughout the dialogue, the passages between the speeches return to this theme, an indication, in Van den Berg's view, that we should use this as a lens through which to read all of the speeches.[41]

Many scholars have noted that the speeches in this dialogue do not add up. There are contradictions within and between speeches delivered by the same person, speakers often go off topic, and logical inconsistencies abound. Van den Berg suggests that these are intentionally included and function to support the message of the dialogue. In Van den Berg's reading it is this method of contradictive argumentation that Tacitus uses throughout to draw attention to his overarching theme. In the same way that his contemporaries make bad assessments of oratory—saying that Secundus and Aper are unskilled when actually they are good models for oratory—so in the speeches, the speakers make bad arguments but still deliver positive proof of the health of oratory in the present age.

To take the first speech as an example, ostensibly what is being debated is the best type of life, the life of a politically active orator versus the life of a retired poet. In his desire to establish the superiority

---

38 Van den Berg, *World of Tacitus' Dialogus*, 102.

39 Ibid., 107.

40 Ibid., 108.

41 Ibid., 98–123.

of the life of the orator, Aper makes a mistake when he draws on the example of the informers, Eprius Marcellus and Vibius Crispus. The point the reader should observe is not that they are bad men but rather that they are both bad illustrating examples for the point that Aper is trying to make.[42] Aper wishes to prove to Maternus that the orator can be self-sufficient but in fact these *delatores* were *not* self-sufficient.[43] They were dependent on the favor of the emperor as the reader would know from their true life histories, from Maternus' objections (13.4) and from Aper's own words (8.3–4). Although Aper uses bad arguments, he himself is actually a good illustration of the point he wants to make: Aper succeeded in his career through merit not the emperor's favor or "traditional venues of power" like office holding.[44] Aper's description of his own career shows one who defends and helps; he does not abuse power (7.1–2; 10.8).[45] When the implications of the inconsistencies in his speech are worked through, the reader is left with the impression that oratory is alive and well in the present age.

Van den Berg's conclusions rest on the identification of a high degree of allusive material in Tacitus and the conviction that Tacitus expects his readers to participate in an intertextual game with him. Right from the first, the characterization of Secundus and Aper draws on Cicero's characterization of Antonius and Crassus in his dialogue, *On the Orator*.[46]

> Yet many ill-naturedly thought that Secundus had no readiness of speech, and that Aper had won his rep-

---

42   In contrast to Gallia, Van den Berg thinks that the readers would not see the *delatores*, Eprius Marcellus and Vibius Crispus as wholly bad. He thinks the *delatores* were not just negative examples in Tacitus' time (38–39). Quintilian, for example, had given Crispus a favorable review in his *Institutes of Oratory* 10.1.119; 12.10.11.

43   Van den Berg, *World of Tacitus'* Dialogus, 131–135.

44   Ibid., 133.

45   Ibid., 128-129; 138–139; see also 129 n. 14.

46   Van den Berg, *World of Tacitus'* Dialogus, 18; dating of the composition and the dramatic date are discussed 31–33.

utation for eloquence by his cleverness and natural powers, more than by training and culture. As a fact, Secundus had a pure, terse, and a sufficiently fluent style, while Aper, who was imbued with learning of all kinds, pretended to despise the culture which he really possessed. He would have, so he must have thought, a greater reputation for industry and application, if it should appear that his genius did not depend on any supports from pursuits alien to his profession (Tacitus, *Dialogue on Oratory* 2.1–2).

There was, if you remember, brother Quintus, a strong persuasion in us when we were boys, that Lucius Crassus had acquired no more learning than he had been enabled to gain from instruction in his youth, and that Marcus Antonius was entirely destitute and ignorant of all erudition whatsoever (Cicero, *On the Orator* 2.1).[47]

But there was such peculiarity in each, that Crassus desired not so much to be thought unlearned as to hold learning in contempt, and to prefer, on every subject, the understanding of our countrymen to that of the Greeks; while Antonius thought that his oratory would be better received by the Roman people if he were believed to have had no learning at all (Cicero, *On the Orator* 2.4).[48]

The benefits of oratory that Aper lists in his first speech (5.5–6) mirror those found in the speech of Crassus in *On the Orator* 1.32. When read in light of this earlier work, Aper's list appears conventional. Similarly, whereas Gallia marks the image of oratory as a weapon in 5.5–6 and draws attention to the disgust this engenders in Maternus (12.2–3), seeing the metaphor as a function of the theme of misuse of power, Van den Berg notes the use of this image

---

47   All translations of this text are taken from Watson.

48   2.1 in Watson.

in Cicero and other authors dating to the first century BCE and first century CE (*On the Orator* 1.32; Pseudo-Cicero, *To Herennius* (*Rhetorica ad Herennium*) 4.38; Quintilian, *Institutes of Oratory* 10.1.30 and 12.9.21), which suggests that the metaphor would not have been shocking to Tacitus' readers but on the contrary, commonplace.[49]

Cicero's dialogues are alluded to in Aper's second speech as well. This speech is about modern style.[50] It is the longest speech in the dialogue which suggests that its topic, the causes and nature of changes in the practice of oratory, are important.[51] Aper's many references to Cicero lead the reader to conclude that Cicero himself, a great orator from the previous age, held an evolutionary theory of oratory (as can be seen in Cicero, *Orator* 1.2; cf. *On the Orator* 3.34 or the catalog of orators in *Brutus*).[52] The fact that oratory today is different from the oratory of the past, Aper argues, is no reason to denigrate it; different does not equate to worse (18.3). Aper focuses on stylistic changes across time rather than on the political circumstances that contributed to the different scope and flavor of oratory in the Republic versus the present period.[53] His arguments go unchallenged in the dialogue and therefore serve to support his contention that modern orators deserve praise.[54]

---

49   Gallia, "*Potentes* and *Potentia*," 176, 181; Van den Berg, *World of Tacitus' Dialogus*, 26, 129–131; on the traditional list of benefits of oratory see also Cicero, *Orator* 141.

50   This speech is discussed in Van den Berg, *World of Tacitus' Dialogus*, 165–179.

51   Ibid., 165–166.

52   Ibid., 232. On the scarcity of good orators throughout history see *On the Orator* 1.9–12; *Brutus* 244.

53   Van den Berg, *World of Tacitus' Dialogus*, 179.

54   Ibid., 167. There are also some minor points on style in this section which can only be appreciated by comparison to earlier works that covered these same topics. One point that Tacitus wants to make in the dialogue, according to Van den Berg, is that orators should utilize poetic language more abundantly, even beyond what Cicero had endorsed (Cicero *On the Orator* 1.158; see also Quintilian, *Institutes of Oratory* 10.1.46–75; 10.1.85–100; on the differences between poetry and oratory see Cicero, *Orator* 68);

Messalla's speech on the education of the orator (the current poor quality of which he sees as being responsible for the contemporary decline in oratory 28.1–3) raises a topic that goes back to Plato and which was also discussed at length in Cicero's dialogues. This section of the dialogue points to Cicero himself as an example of a learned orator and alludes to Cicero's description of the ideal educational program, mentioning his dialogue, *Brutus*, by name.[55]

> [B]ut I will first recall your attention to the training which we have been told was practised by those orators whose infinite industry, daily study and incessant application to every branch of learning are seen in the contents of their own books. You are doubtless familiar with Cicero's book, called Brutus. In the latter part of it (the first gives an account of the ancient orators) he relates his own beginnings, his progress, and the growth, so to say, of his eloquence. ... The truth indeed is this, my excellent friends, that Cicero's wonderful eloquence wells up and overflows out of a store of erudition, a multitude of accomplishments, and a knowledge that was universal. The strength and power of oratory, unlike all other arts, is not confined within narrow and straitened limits, but the orator is he who can speak on every question with grace, elegance, and persuasiveness, suitably to the dignity of his subject, the requirements of the occasion, and the taste of his audience (30.2–5).

discussed in Van den Berg, 171–172, 226–231. In Van den Berg's reading, poetry, a common theme in dialogue, appears once again, this time in regard to its proper use in the practice of public speaking. Our third reading, to which we turn next, will see a different type of emphasis on poetry in Tacitus' dialogue.

55 Cicero in *On the Orator* wrote that the orator should have a good knowledge of all important subjects (see especially 1.20; 3.54–55) but that they only need to learn as much as is practical, that is, enough to enable them to persuade an audience (see for example 1.21–22, 221–222; 3.86–90); see also *Orator* 113–122. Van den Berg also includes comparisons to Quintilian's theories on oratorical education, 183–186.

Aper had argued for a developmental schema; Messalla sees antiquity as the standard by which all other periods should be evaluated.[56] In appealing to Cicero's description of the proper education for an orator, Messalla is here appealing to an ideal rather than to what was actually happening in the Republic. Even so, the discerning reader would recognize that Aper himself, imbued as he was "with learning of all kinds" (2.2), still proves that orators of the present generation could meet the high standards of that earlier age.[57]

In Van den Berg's reading of the dialogue, making identification between narrator and author is an important component of the reader's experience. Tacitus' own life, as was mentioned briefly at the start of this chapter, was a proof that Roman orators could still engage in cases of import. Pliny and Tacitus prosecuted Marius Priscus, governor of Africa, for corruption and cruelty (*repetundae*; see Pliny, *Letters* 2.11 and 2.12 and Juvenal 1.47–50).[58] In Pliny's description of this trial, he mentions several times that the case was drawing in the crowds and was perceived to be a trial of much moment.[59]

In this intertextual reading, Tacitus' attitude toward the imperial government and the *principate* is not a concern. A central question of the dialogue is rather whether there could be good oratory in the present time.[60] The dialogue consequently provides good evidence for the role of rhetoric in the imperial era as well as of the perception of that role rather than serving as a strong evidence base for Tacitus' political views.[61]

---

56   Van den Berg, *World of Tacitus' Dialogus*, 181.

57   Ibid., 185.

58   Van den Berg, *World of Tacitus' Dialogus*, 30–31, 189–190.

59   Ibid., 74–76 and 84–85.

60   Ibid., 207.

61   Ibid., 50.

Third Reading: An Anti-*principate* Reading

In this reading by Shadi Bartsch,[62] Tacitus is understood to be giving us an anti-*princeps* message in the dialogue. The contradictions in the speeches are evidence of "doublespeak"—a multivalent way of writing which allows the individual reader to interpret the message as being either anti- or pro-*princeps* depending on the personal inclination of the reader.[63] Tacitus must not, for safety's sake, openly criticize the present emperor or the office itself and so he distances himself, as he needs to, with doublespeak.

On literary grounds, Bartsch thinks that the dialogue was written during the reign of Nerva.[64] He points out that under Nerva, informers such as those mentioned in the first set of speeches, Marcellus and Crispus, who had flourished under earlier, "bad" emperors were in no way punished or held to account once a benevolent emperor had assumed control of the state. We can see this in the writings of Pliny the Younger. Pliny relates an anecdote about a dinner party at which the topic of conversation was the infamous informer, Catullus Messalinus, who had flourished under Domitian. The honest Junius Mauricus pointed out to Emperor Nerva that if Messalinus were still alive, he would surely be among the invited guests (*Letter* 4.22.4–6). Informers went on from reign to reign regardless of who was emperor. What for Gallia were two separate points of critique (*princeps* versus imperial *delatores*), Bartsch collapses. In Bartsch's reading, Tacitus believes that the whole Roman government is broken and corrupt. A system that puts one man at the helm creates a situation in which all revolves around the will and favor of one individual. Such a system is conducive to corruption. But it was unsafe for Tacitus to state this openly. Any critique of

---

62   Shadi Bartsch, "Praise and Doublespeak: Tacitus' *Dialogus*," in *Oxford Readings in Tacitus*, ed. Rhiannon Ash (Oxford: Oxford University Press, 2012), 119–154; updated repr. of chapter 4 of *Actors in the Audience* (Cambridge, MA: Harvard University Press,1994).

63   Ibid., 140.

64   For the bibliography on this see Ibid., 149 n. 75; date of the composition is covered, 149–154.

the *principate* had to be constructed in such a way that a more positive view of the *principate* was possible. Bartsch thinks that some readers will even have wanted to extract a positive message from the dialogue. Living in the age of a good emperor, Nerva, many of his readers may not have agreed with Tacitus' negative assessment of the present system of government.

As in the reading of Gallia, so in Bartsch's reading of the dialogue, the links between the persons mentioned in the dialogue and their true life histories are factors that should be used to help us interpret the speeches and their meaning. Several characters are presented as, or were known to be, champions of political liberty. Helvidius Priscus is described as someone whom the informer Marcellus had recently defeated (5.7). Helvidius Priscus' exile and death occurred at approximately the same time as the dramatic date of the *Dialogue*.[65] Helvidius Priscus had attempted to put down the power of the *delatores*, especially that of Marcellus; Marcellus and Crispus were ranged against Priscus and Marcellus had been involved in the prosecution of Priscus' father-in-law, Thrasea, himself a champion of Republican liberty.[66]

Allusions to the historical Cato the Younger are also key to uncovering the message of the dialogue. In 46 BCE, Cato had committed suicide rather than live in a state subservient to the will of Julius Caesar (Plutarch, *Life of Cato the Younger* 66; 69–73; see also Lucan, *Pharsalia* 9.19–30, 253–293). Marcellus links Cato to Helvetius Priscus in *Histories* 4.8 and Maternus himself has just written a tragedy entitled *Cato*.[67]

---

65 Bartsch, "Praise and Doublespeak," 130; for bibliography on this see nn.23 and 25.

66 *Histories* 4.4–10 and 4.43; *Annals* 16.28–29; see also *Agricola* 2.1; on Thraesa see *Agricola* 2.1; *Annals* 16.21–22, 34–35; *Histories* 4.5–8; Juvenal, *Satire* 5.36; and Plutarch, *Life of Cato the Younger* 25.1; 37.1.

67 Ibid., 129. The historical identify of Maternus is "unrecoverable" but Bartsch goes through the options for the historical person of Maternus (123–124). One Maternus was put to death for declaiming against tyrants (Cassius Dio 67.12.5).

Maternus could be intended as a parallel with Socrates in Plato's *Phaedo* (which dialogue is set on the eve of his death) or with Crassus in *On the Orator* (in which dialogue it is noted that the dramatic date of the dialogue is just before the death of Crassus 3.1; see also 3.9–12).[68] These parallels strengthen the characterization of Maternus as a champion of liberty as well as one who was doomed to fall victim to an oppressive state. Maternus in his last speech alludes to the words of Cicero in *Brutus* 45 (as has been mentioned in all three interpretations). But Bartsch sees a relationship between *Brutus* as a whole and the themes of Tacitus' dialogue. The *Brutus* is a dialogue about the decline of oratory due to a lack of freedom (since the rise of Julius Caesar; *Brutus* 9; 22; 331). Cicero laments Brutus' lack of opportunities in a state that has morphed into a dictatorship:

> [A]nd whenever I see you, my Brutus, I am concerned to think where your wonderful genius, your finished erudition, and unparalleled industry will find a theatre to display themselves. For after you had thoroughly improved your abilities by pleading a variety of important causes, and when my declining vigor was just giving way and lowering the ensigns of dignity to your more active talents, the liberty of the state received a fatal overthrow, and that eloquence, of which we are now to give the history, was condemned to perpetual silence (*Brutus* 22).[69]

In Bartsch's reading, what the reader should realize is that Cicero and Maternus agree that great oratory requires freedom from absolute rule.[70]

In addition to reading the dialogue with its generic precedents in mind, Bartsch analyzes the dialogue as a discrete literary work,

---

68   Bartsch, "Praise and Doublespeak,"124; for bibliography on this see 124–125 n. 12.

69   *Brutus* 6 in Watson.

70   Bartsch, "Praise and Doublespeak," 131–132.

noting the significance of language and structure. In Bartsch's view, Maternus' comments on liberty, license, and eloquence are instances of doublespeak.[71] He compares the language of Maternus in 27.3 and 40.2. In 27.3, Maternus gives us the clue as to how to read the final speech when he states that freedom of speech is no more (27.3: "Proceed," said Maternus, "As you are speaking of the ancients, avail yourself of ancient freedom, from which we have fallen away even yet more than from eloquence"). The take-away here, according to Bartsch, is that Maternus himself is not free to speak openly so that when he appears to speak favorably of present conditions in the speech in 40 (it was the *Republican* era government which was problematic, unruly and mistaking license for liberty), we should look for hidden meanings.[72] In addition, the beginning and end of the dialogue operate to interpret each other. The first debate (political life versus retired life) is crucial because it "reveals ... the political conditions of the times" which we must then apply to the interpretation of the last half.[73] Maternus in his focus on poetry shows us that under the current political conditions of the *principate* only the poet can attack the powerful. The poet essentially replaces the republican orator of old as poetry becomes the new vehicle for free speech.[74] It is through his tragedy that Maternus intends to strike out at the state. Bartsch concludes that the *Dialogue* is really "*about* the transition of political comment from one realm to another: it is about how the conditions of the principate have encouraged the indirect medium of poetry to take over from the forthright voice of oratory."[75]

Maternus, in Bartsch's view, operates as a mouthpiece for Tacitus. Throughout Tacitus' writings a repeating motif is that literary works that criticize the ruling power can lead to death or punishment by the state. Cremutius Cordus, for example, discussed in the

---

71   Ibid., 143.

72   Bartsch, "Praise and Doublespeak," 137.

73   Ibid., 147.

74   Ibid., 142–143.

75   Ibid., 144.

Annals, had published a history in which he had praised the assassins of Julius Caesar (*Annals* 4.34–35; the language of liberty and license is present in his speech before the Senate). The opening of *Agricola* mentions that it was a capital crime to read the panegyrics composed on Priscus Helvidius (mentioned by Aper) and his father-in-law Thrasea (*Agricola* 2.1–3).[76]

And it is not only the themes of Tacitus' *Dialogue on Oratory* that occur in his other works but also the same "doublespeak" method itself.[77] As an example Bartsch points to the opening of the *Agricola*, where Tacitus writes:

> Now at last our spirit is returning. And yet, though at the dawn of a most happy age Nerva Cæsar blended things once irreconcilable, sovereignty and freedom, though Nerva Trajan is now daily augmenting the prosperity of the time, ... Yet we shall not regret that we have told, though in language unskillful and unadorned, the story of past servitude, and borne our testimony to present happiness. Meanwhile this book, intended to do honour to Agricola, my father-in-law, will, as an expression of filial regard, be commended, or at least excused. (*Agricola* 3.1–3; see also *Histories* 1.1)[78]

In the first and third interpretations presented above, Tacitus' aim is primarily political, though these two readings differ as to what that message is. In these, we understand Tacitus best by understanding the characters in the frame. His aim in the second, intertextual, reading is not primarily political and he is best understood with reference to his literary predecessors. In this second reading, the dialogue is used as a means of assessing the state of oratory in the imperial age: by comparing and contrasting what the speakers have to say about the courts with contemporary sources the author

---

76   Ibid., 125.

77   Ibid., 141 n. 54.

78   Taken from the Church and Brodribb 1899 translation.

shows that orators did have much business to conduct in this time. As we can see in this example, familiarity with the conventions of the genre of dialogue does not automatically lead us to uncover its real message and its potential. But it does allow us to look beyond the surface and it opens up possibilities.

CHAPTER III

SECOND SOPHISTIC AND CHRISTIAN DIALOGUE

In the late first, second, and third centuries, dialogue expanded in different directions. This period witnessed not only the continuation of the philosophical dialogue along Platonic and Ciceronian lines (in the writings of Plutarch) but also the development of a new type of dialogue called "table-talk," (Plutarch, Athenaeus, and Methodius), comedic dialogue (Lucian), and Christian dialogue (Justin Martyr, Octavius Felix, and Methodius). The works of two prolific dialogue authors, Plutarch and Lucian, are best understood in relation to the Second Sophistic movement. The writings of the first extant Christian dialogist, Justin Martyr, are best understood as an attempt to articulate a distinct Christian identity. This chapter will survey the dialogues of Plutarch and Lucian briefly and analyze in detail Justin Martyr's *Dialogue with Trypho*.

From the late first century to the third century CE there was an explosion of Greek literature. These writings, though spanning many established genres and even creating new ones, shared a respect for the inherited culture of Greece. By the post-Hellenic period, certain authors of the Archaic and Classical period had become in effect a canon. Second Sophistic writers viewed these writings as authoritative and their own intellectual and literary contributions were formed in relation to them.

Plutarch (lived c. 46–120 CE) was a priest of Delphi and prolific author. He wrote biographies of famous Greek and Roman men but also a hodgepodge of treaties, essays, and dialogues which today we designate by the term *Moralia*. The writings in this collection address philosophical, religious, political, and literary themes.

We have mentioned that we can divide Plutarch's dialogues into two main types, the traditional philosophical type and the sympotic ("table-talk") variety. Within the former category, Plutarch used a variety of structures and characters. This is true too, of the writings of Lucian, our next dialogist, and probably reflects the genre's expansion. Most of the philosophical dialogues of Plutarch are depicted as being conducted amicably and they resemble the constructive Platonic or Ciceronian dialogue in that there is usually one dominant speaker, or the speakers take it in turn to speak each at length, and the speakers tend to come to an agreement. In *Against the Stoics*, for example, the interlocutor asks for more information rather than presenting challenging questions or asking for a different viewpoint (as at 1066d). In *On the Delays of the Divine Vengeance* 548b–c, the participants at the outset of the dialogue agree that Epicurus' views were outrageously misguided and they determine amongst themselves to argue against his idea that there is a delay in divine justice (cp. *That Epicurus Actually Makes a Pleasant Life Impossible*).[1]

Dialogues often record conversations that took place earlier (for example, *Table-Talk*; *Concerning the Face which Appears in the Orb of the Moon*; *The Dialogue on Love*; and *The E at Delphi*). Participants in the dialogues can be historical persons (*The Dinner of the Seven*

---

1   In *The Oracles at Delphi No Longer Given in Verse* the participants agree with and add to each other's comments (see 402e). In *On the Control of Anger* most of the talking is done by Fundanus and Sulla's role is merely to urge him to speak at the outset of the piece and to this we can compare *Reply to Colotes in Defense of the Other Philosophers* in which Plutarch is set up to be the main speaker. We do not see the dialogue participants disagreeing on important points of philosophy, ethics, or religion. In *The E at Delphi* the interlocutors take it in turn to speak and there is no resolution but uncertainty over the meaning of the E at Delphi that does not translate into uncertainty over the religious truths behind this inscription. In some dialogues there is no agreed upon resolution but the issue at stake is trivial as in *Table-Talk*, Book One, Question 2 in which the question is: at a dinner party, should the host assign seats or should the guests be left to choose a seat for themselves? There are four different views given, including that of Plutarch (1.615e–619a). The speakers take it in turn to speak. The final word is given by Lamprias who disagrees with Plutarch (1.617f–619a). Yet even in this case agreement is the end result as everyone agrees to give Lamprias leave to arrange their own party as he chooses (1.618d).

Wise Men); Plutarch's family and friends; or fictional characters who stand for something. In *On the Delays of the Divine Vengeance* Plutarch himself, his son-in-law Patrocleas, and his brother Timon are participants; the character "Epicurus" is not the historical Epicurus but rather stands in for Epicurean views, and the character Thespesius' name is similarly suspect as the word means "divine things."[2]

Sometimes Plutarch is not the ostensible narrator or is not depicted as being present (*The Dinner of the Seven Wise Men*; *On the Control of Anger*; *Beasts Are Rational*; *The Oracles at Delphi No Longer Given in Verse*; and *The Obsolescence of Oracles* where the "I" is Lamprias, Plutarch's brother).

Plutarch shows an affinity for more than one philosophical school in his work, Stoic, Pythagorean, and Aristotelian. He was a Platonist and Platonism by his day did incorporate elements of other schools so this should not surprise us.[3] He wrote several dialogues with philosophical themes: *Reply to Colotes in Defence of the Other Philosophers*; *On the Delays of the Divine Vengeance*; *Against the Stoics*; *Dialogue on Love*; *On the Control of Anger*; *That Epicurus Actually Makes a Pleasant Life Impossible* (on pleasure); and *Whether Vice Be Sufficient to Cause Unhappiness* (a possible dialogue, fragmentary). From these titles we can see that he took up many of the same themes that were discussed in Platonic or Ciceronian dialogues (justice, love, and the happy life).

Several of Plutarch's non-dialogue works also cover themes seen in the philosophical dialogues of Plato and Cicero such as virtue (*Virtue and Vice*; *Progress in Virtue*; *On Moral Virtue*; and *Can*

---

2   *On the Sign of Socrates* includes historical personages but also persons created to stand for types such as the Timarchus of the myth or the Pythagorean Theanor whose name meant "man of god"; in *The Oracles at Delphi No Longer Given in Verse* Boëthus is a historical personage who is already at the time of the dialogue a burgeoning Epicurean; in *Table-Talk* 5.673c he is a mouthpiece for Epicurean views.

3   John Dillon, "Plutarch and Platonism," in *A Companion to Plutarch*, ed. Mark Beck (Malden, MA: Wiley Blackwell, 2014), 61.

Virtue Be Taught?); the nature of the soul (*On the Generation of the Soul in Timaeus*; on the irrational and rational soul, see *On Moral Virtue* 441e–442c; 443b–d); sense perception (*Life of Demetrius*; *Concerning the Face which Appears in the Orb of the Moon*; and *On the Principle of Cold*); and states and state-craft (*Precepts of Statecraft*; *To an Uneducated Ruler*; *On Monarchy, Democracy, and Oligarchy*; *Whether an Old Man Should Engage in Public Affairs*; and *That a Philosopher Ought to Converse Especially with Men in Power*).

His views on mimesis and poetry expressed in these non-dialogue works are important because they relate to his dialogues on religion. In *Progress in Virtue* 84c, we can see that Plutarch accepts the commonly held idea that people take others as their model. In his view, poetry may be admired for imitating realistically even bad persons or acts but the young reader must be careful to distinguish admiration of the technique from admiration of the model (*How to Read Poetry* 17f–18f).[4] Plutarch compares poetry and wrong reading with religion and wrong thinking (*How to Read Poetry* 26b).[5] Though it can contain moral messages, poetry is described as being liable to misunderstandings and therefore dangerous for the young to read without a guide.

Plutarch does not have one clear theory on the value of poetry for promoting a right understanding of the gods. If we take all of his comments together and try to harmonize them, then we might say that he sees poetry as a potential repository for truths about the gods but one that is inferior to other types of religious repositories. Mystery cults for example offer better expressions of truths about the gods than poetry. The mythic tales of Isis and Osiris for example are not like the fabrications of poets and prose but superior to them:

---

4   *Mimesis* in Plutarch is discussed in L. Van der Stockt, *Twinkling and Twilight: Plutarch's Reflections on Literature* (Brussels: Paleis der Academiën, 1992), 21–55.

5   Plutarch would view the religious dread described in this passage as superstition, see his *Superstition*, especially 167d–f; Peter van Nuffelen, *Rethinking the Gods: Philosophical Readings of Religion in the Post-Hellenistic Period* (Cambridge: Cambridge University Press, 2011), 169.

And yet that these relations are nothing akin to those foppish tales and vain fictions which poets and story-tellers are wont, like spiders, to spin out of their own bowels, without any substantial ground or foundation for them, and then weave and wire-draw them out at their own pleasures, but contain in them certain abstruse questions and rehearsals of events, you yourself are, I suppose, convinced (*Isis and Osiris* 358f).[6]

Poetry was taken up by Second Sophistic authors because it was part of the received Hellenic tradition and like religion, as we will see below, was part of what made Greeks Greek after they had lost their political independence. Other Second Sophistic philosophers discuss the ability of poetry to provide correct religious knowledge.[7]

Plutarch wrote several dialogues that have religious themes: *The E at Delphi*; *The Oracles at Delphi No Longer Given in Verse*; *The Obsolescence of Oracles*; *On the Delays of the Divine Vengeance*. He was a priest at Delphi but he also wrote with insider knowledge on the mystery cult of Isis and Osiris (*Isis and Osiris*, a non-dialogue work) and he took a keen interest in divination which is reflected not only in the dialogues concerning the Delphic oracle but also in *On the Sign of Socrates* 581b–582c, and 588c–594a. Simon Swain has suggested that the search for divine authority reflected in Second Sophistic writings was part of the search for the best Greek models. Philosophers saw it as their job to help provide correct

---

6   This translation taken from *Plutarch's Morals*, trans. William W. Goodwin, vol. 4 (Boston: Little, Brown and Company, 1878); in Goodwin's numbering this is *Isis and Osiris* 20; discussed in Van Nuffelen, *Rethinking the Gods*, 58. In some of Plutarch's works, poetry is not seen as corrupting as it was in Plato (3).

7   In Dio Chrysostom, *Olympic Discourse* 40–41 some poets get it wrong; in *Borysthenitic Discourse* 33–35 poets do not get everything wrong but, not having the requisite knowledge, they are not able to get everything right; in Philostratus, *Apollonius of Tyana* 5.14.2–3 poets misrepresent the gods in dangerous way (fables do not—they are conducive to philosophy); see also Lucian below.

Hellenic religious belief and practice.[8] We find such ideas in the writings of the Greek orator Dio Chrysostom (c. 40 CE–c. 115 CE). In *Olympic Discourse* 47, philosophers are a source of knowledge of the deities and perhaps the most perfect. Philosophers dedicate themselves to truth, wisdom, and the care and cultivation of the gods (Dio Chrysostom, *On Philosophy* 7). Philostratus (c. 170/172–247/250 CE) in his biography of the philosopher and holy man, Apollonius of Tyana, likewise shares these views. In that work, Apollonius describes his philosophy (his wisdom, *sophia*) as "an inspiration ... which teaches men how to pray and sacrifice to the gods" (4.40.1; see also 4.44.2).[9] Apollonius, like Plutarch, was engaged in expounding right religious beliefs and practices (Philostratus, *Apollonius of Tyana* 1.1.2; 1.16.3; 4.1.2). He instructed cities; Plutarch his readers (see especially his non-dialogue work, *Superstition*, which defines true religion as lying in between atheism and superstition).

In the Second Sophistic era, then, religion and philosophy were seen as two ways of reaching truth. The goddess Isis for example is said to be a lover of wisdom and those who are devout worshippers at her shrine will be able to comprehend reality (*Isis and Osiris* 351f–352a). The truly devout will use reason to understand the truths behind the ceremonies of the mystery cult (352c). Plutarch's self-imposed task was to help others get to that philosophical truth contained within traditional religion through correct interpretation and he often used the dialogue form to do this.[10]

---

8   Simon Swain, "Defending Hellenism: Philostratus, *In Honour of Apollonius*," in *Apologetics in the Roman Empire: Pagans, Jews, and Christians*, eds. Mark J. Edwards, Martin Goodman, and Simon Price, in association with Christopher Rowland (Oxford: Clarendon Press, 1999), 161–162, 167–168, 172–173.

9   Translation taken from Philostratus. *The Life of Apollonius of Tyana, The Epistles of Apollonius and the Treatise of Eusebius*, trans. F. C. Conybeare, vol. 1 (London: William Heinemann; New York: Macmillan, 1912).

10 See Van Nuffelen, *Rethinking the Gods*, 4, 49, 55, 61. Van Nuffelen has identified two major themes in the philosophical writings of the time of Plutarch: 1) Religion was created by the wise ancients and contains philosophical knowledge; 2) The religious pantheon is a perfect hierarchy and

Table-Talk

In the Hellenistic period, the dialogue was associated with the symposium, or the convivial dining experience. The symposium was an environment in which Greek men or Greek-educated men, worked through, and put on display, Greek culture, in the intimate setting of a dinner among peers. The practice of holding and attending symposia was essentially a form of "cultural identity construction."[11] The Romans were familiar with Hellenistic examples of the sympotic dialogue as well Plato, Xenophon, and Aristotle.[12]

The Plutarchian corpus includes this type of dialogue. In his collection of sympotic conversations, Plutarch calls this the sixth book of his "table-talk" (6.686e; see also *The Dinner of the Seven Wise Men*). At the start of Book 1, he lists as his predecessors in the genre Plato, Xenophon, Aristotle, Speusippus, Epicurus, Prytanis, Hieronymus, and Dio of the Academy (*Table-Talk* 1.612d–e). The latest of these figures dates to the end of the third century BCE which fact suggests that perhaps Plutarch was reviving this form of the genre after a long break in the tradition.[13]

In *Table-Talk*, Book 1 in the preface, Plutarch sets up the proposed series of writings. He will record the worthwhile, learned discussions, which he has had with dinner companions both at Rome and in Greece. Each book is to be arranged by 10 questions. The topics are wide-ranging and the method of recording them varies. Sometimes he but summarizes the different views expressed

---

model for the ordering of human society and all "levels of being." Plutarch, like other philosophers, rejects any philosophical interpretations other than his own; they may some of them be partially correct but his own are always best; see also the essay by Rainer Hirsch-Luipold, "Religion and Myth," trans. Mark Beck, in *Companion to Plutarch*, 163–176.

11 Goldhill, "Introduction," 3–4.

12 For an overview of the trajectory of Roman dialogues, see Powell, "Dialogues and Treatises," 223–240.

13 Jason König, *Saints and Symposiasts: The Literature of Food and the Symposium in Greco-Roman and Early Christian Cult*ure (Cambridge: Cambridge University Press, 2012), 12, 16.

(1.619b–f), sometimes he uses the dialogue form. Proper etiquette for hosts and guests is a common theme but there were also discussions of historical queries, the natural world, and medicine. Jason König, in his study of sympotic literature, notes two overarching foci, what we might call "social knowledge" (correct sympotic behavior) and literary eruditeness (displays of knowledge).[14]

Plato is sometimes the starting point (see for example, 8.718c: What did Plato mean by saying that God is always doing geometry?). The talk is reminiscent of Platonic dialogues in terms of the topics covered and the method of discussing them. The speakers begin with a topic but then try to get behind that question to the premises or fundamentals that would affect it (see for example 1.613c–d). Plutarch ostensibly intends for his real self to be equated with the "I" of the dialogue. He is not taking on a persona but purports to be recounting real conversations that happened. He is writing to a real person, one Senecio, who is known from the historical record. None of these facts however prove that these conversations ever actually took place. Even if Plutarch took notes at a dinner party they must have been summary and the most that he could do would be to relay the general sense of any arguments made.[15] In the later examples of table-talk that developed after Plutarch in the writings of Athenaeus (end of the second and beginning of the third century CE) and Macrobius (early fifth century CE) it is clear that the conversations are literary constructs.

The models of Plato, Xenophon, and the Hellenistic examples set the structure and the topics. We can see the same string of topics in sympotic works from all of these periods: food, things one does at or after a dinner (see Athenaeus, *The Learned Banqueters* (*Deipnosophists*) 15.665d for example) and sex (discussed in Xenophon, *Symposium* 9.7; Plutarch, *Table-Talk* 3.653b–655d); Athenaeus, Book 13).[16] In

---

14   Ibid., 8, 9, 11, 39.

15   Pliny the Elder was said to have taken or dictated notes on literary works while at dinner (Pliny the Younger, *Letter* 3.5.12-13).

16   See John Wilkins, "Dialogue and Comedy: The Structure of the Deipnosophistae," in *Athenaeus and His World: Reading Greek Culture in*

Second Sophistic and Late Antiquity versions, the point is to play with these established themes and topics and for the authors to contribute their own learned opinion. One recurring theme is whether food or learned discourse should be the real focus of the symposium. In Lucian's *Lexiphanes*, the character from which the dialogue takes its name presents his own literary *Symposium* in which the focus is entirely on satisfying the bodily desires (6–8; 13–15); the dinner guests are similarity not interested in philosophical discourse in Lucian's *Symposium*.[17] Romeri suggests that in Plutarch the discourse is most important but in Athenaeus's writings he wants to show that the pleasures of body and mind are equally important.[18] There is a strong element of competition that takes place in the literary depictions of the table-talk dialogues in the conversations between the participants (and which reflects actual social practice). This element of one-up-man-ship is mirrored by the author's desire to surpass the earlier table-talk writings. We can see Athenaeus doing this in his work with regard to Plato. He uses a Platonic model to try and surpass that model (for example of critiques of Plato see 11.504c–509c).[19]

Plutarch's dialogues are full of social, intellectual, philosophical, and religious history. We see in his works, a new generation engaging with the themes of earlier dialogues, adding new ones, and pushing the pre-existing boundaries of the genre (in the form of table-talk). Lucian will produce new configurations of the genre and exuberantly manipulate the classical canon to mock the themes and

---

the *Roman Empire*, eds. David Braund, and John Wilkins, foreword by Glen Bowerstock (Exeter: University of Exeter Press, 2000), 28–29; so Graham Anderson, "The Banquet of Belles-Lettres: Athenaeus and the Comic Symposium," in *Athenaeus and His World: Reading Greek Culture in the Roman Empire*, eds. David Braund, and John Wilkins, foreword by Glen Bowerstock (Exeter: University of Exeter Press, 2000), 322.

17   Luciana Romeri, "The λογόδειπνον: Athenaeus between Banquet and Anti-Banquet," trans. Kerensa Pearson in *Athenaeus and His World: Reading Greek Culture in the Roman Empire*, eds. David Braund, and John Wilkins, foreword by Glen Bowerstock (Exeter: University of Exeter Press, 2000), 260–262.

18   Ibid., 269–270.

19   Discussed in Wilkins, "Dialogue and Comedy," 23–24.

methods of his Second Sophistic contemporaries.

Comic Dialogues

Lucian lived ~125–180 CE.[20] We know little of his personal life. His claim to fame rests entirely on his many entertaining works. Both Lucian's dialogues and his other works were hybrid creations which he and his contemporaries described as having a novel freshness (*Zeuxis* 1; *Dionysus* 5).[21] Lucian draws on different genres and themes, utilizing them and altering them as best suits his purpose which was to transform the received tradition in creative and entertaining ways.[22] An example of the way in which Lucian mixes genres is his *Alexander the False Prophet*, which has been described as an "epistolary biography ... consisting of narrative, comic dialogue, and many oracles."[23] Many of his works are parodies of established genres: *True Story* is a parody of traveler's tales; *On the Syrian Goddess* is a parody of Herodotus' descriptions of exotic cults; *Gout* is a parody of tragedy; *Dialogue of the Courtesans* is a parody of New Comedy.[24]

If we confine ourselves to the dialogues, we can see that Lucian exhibits a great variety of style. He has dialogues which feature recounted tales of journeys to other worlds (his Menippean satires

---

20 On the impossibility of dating of Lucian's works, see Jennifer Hall, *Lucian's Satire*, rev. ed. (New York: Arno Press, 1981), 44–47.

21 On the hybrid nature of Lucian's works see Tim Whitmarsh, *Greek Literature and the Roman Empire: The Politics of Imitation* (Oxford: Oxford University Press, 2001), 75–77.

22 Adam Bartley, "Techniques of Composition in Lucian's Minor Dialogues," *Hermes* 133 (2005): 359.

23 R. Bracht Branham, "The Comic as Critic: Revenging Epicurus: A Study of Lucian's Art of Comic Narrative," *Classical Antiquity* 3.2 (1984): 150.

24 *Menippus* (*Necyomantia*) is a parody of Odysseus' descent to the Underworld in the Odyssey Book 11; for *On the Syrian Goddess*, see J. L. Lightfoot, ed., *Lucian. On the Syrian Goddess* (Oxford: Oxford University Press, 2003); on *Dialogue of the Courtesans* see R. Bracht Branham, *Unruly Eloquence: Lucian and the Comedy of Traditions* (Cambridge, MA: Harvard University Press, 1989), 128.

on which see below). He has dialogues in which the exchanges between speakers is limited and can comprise a few paragraphs only (such as the *Dialogues of the Gods*). He also has dialogues in which there is sustained philosophical discussion (such as *Hermotimus*).

The dialogues are hard to categorize neatly. They are moving away from traditional models which complicates matters. The most traditional in terms of its structure and content is *Hermotimus* in which the Platonic model is most closely adhered to. This is a dialogue between the Stoic Hermotimus and Lycinus (which name appears in several dialogues and which may or may not represent Lucian himself). To this we might compare *The Cynic*, a dialogue in which Lycinus challenges a Cynic (if this work is indeed by Lucian, a matter of some dispute).

Lucian uses fictional characters, personifications ("Frankness," or "Dialogue" for example), and also real persons (such as Alexander and Peregrinus, both religious figures of the second century CE). Several of the dialogues have a Cynic or Skeptic as the narrator or primary speaker. Diogenes of Sinope (the fourth century founder of the Cynics) and Menippus, a Hellenistic Cynic, are recurring dialogue protagonists. Menippus lived in the first half of the third century BCE and was the inventor of a new type of satire, a seriocomical prose-verse mix (Diogenes Laertius 6.99–101; Strabo, *Geography* 16.2.29; Marcus Aurelius, *Meditations* 6.47). Lucian wrote two Menippean satires, *Icaromenippus* and *Menippus* (*Necyomantia*) and Lucian himself draws attention to the Menippean or Cynic influence on his dialogues in two of his works, *Double Indictment* 33 (Menippus and Cynics) and *The Fisherman* 26 (Menippus).[25] In *The Fisherman*, the philosophers whom Lucian has vilified in his dialogues attack and Lucian finds himself on trial for his life. Diogenes serves as a prosecutor:

> Worst of all, Philosophy, he shelters himself under

---

25 Joel C. Relihan, *Ancient Menippean Satire* (Baltimore, MD: Johns Hopkins University Press, 1993), 103–118 notes that he adapts the genre in *Dialogues of the Dead* and *Zeus Rants*.

your name, entices Dialogue from our company to be his ally and mouthpiece, and induces our good comrade Menippus to collaborate constantly with him; Menippus, more by token, is the one deserter and absentee on this occasion (*The Fisherman* 26).[26]

We might be tempted to conclude that in so far as Lucian promotes an ideal character or way of life, he promotes the ideal of the Menippean figure (Menippus ostensibly appears as such in *Dialogues of the Dead* and in *Menippus*). But we should be cautious for whether we are considering the corpus as a whole or an individual work, the Menippean or Cynic viewpoint is often undercut. The feature characteristic of Menippean satire is that it refuses to take anything seriously and even the author or narrator himself is called into question.[27] In *Menippus* for example, the narrator, Menippus, travels to the Hades in order to learn the best way to live. He rejects the philosophers of earth and he endorses a life of simplicity (4). But Menippus is comically depicted from the very the outset and the bizarre appearance and versified speech of this character disrupt the moral message of his outrageous tale, as does his emergence at the end of the piece from the oracle of Trophonius, since Lucian elsewhere characterizes oracles as a type of false authority (*Menippus* 1; 22).[28]

Menippean satire was a logical choice for Lucian because it rejects authoritative answers. Such works also frequently parody other types of genres, particularly "sober modes of discourse" or didactic genres and it may be this feature rather than any desire to promote a particular mode of life that influenced Lucian to add it to his

---

26   Unless otherwise noted, all translations of Lucian are taken from *The Works of Lucian of Samosata*, trans. H. W. Fowler, and F.G. Fowler, vol. 1 (Oxford Clarendon Press, 1905).

27   Relihan, *Ancient Menippean Satire*, 20, 22.

28   On the oracle of Trophonius see *Dialogues of the Dead*, dialogue between Menippus, Amphilochus, and Trophonius; Branham, *Unruly Eloquence*, 20, 21; Reilhan, *Ancient Menippean Satire*, 104–114.

literary mix.[29] Reilhan describes it this way:

> We shall see that we have to deal with an intellectual joke, which in its origins is not concerned with finding new ways to truth but only with making fun of those who would claim to have found it, or who would try to preach it. Menippus is a mocker, and those who follow in his footsteps mock themselves and their own works: the creation of a work of literature is itself a violation of the cardinal principle that there can be no authoritative point of view about anything important.[30]

It would be more proper to say that Lucian had a thematic interest in mocking the "folly of human desires" and especially concern for wealth (*The Ship*; *Voyage to the Lower World*; *Nigrinus*; *Dialogues of the Dead Charon*; *Menippus*) rather than offering a positive rule for conduct.[31]

Lucian's targets (philosophy, myth, and literary critics) were not new but his approach and his form were revolutionary. In some of his works he tells us what he is doing, the new form that he is trying to create, and what he hopes to achieve with it. In *Double Indictment* 33–34 Lucian indicates that he is drawing on Old Comedy, the Cynic tradition, and Menippus. In 33, the character "Dialogue" complains that Lucian has transformed him:

> Whisking off the seemly tragic mask I then wore, he clapped on in its place a comic one that was little short of ludicrous: his next step was to huddle me into a corner with Jest, Lampoon, Cynicism, and the comedians Eupolis and Aristophanes, persons with a horrible

---

29 Reilhan, *Ancient Menippean Satire*, 25, 35.

30 Ibid.,17.

31 Bartley, "Techniques of Composition," 360. Some of his dialogues lamented inequalities as we see in *Timon* in which work, which parallels Aristophanes play, *Plutus,* the blindness of the god allows the undeserving to be rich (*Saturnalia* and the *Correspondence with Cronus* also touch on this theme).

knack of making light of sacred things, and girding at all that is as it should be. But the climax was reached when he unearthed a barking, snarling old Cynic, Menippus by name, and thrust *his* company upon me; a grim bulldog, if ever there was one; a treacherous brute that will snap at you while his tail is yet wagging. Could any man be more abominably misused? Stripped of my proper attire, I am made to play the buffoon, and to give expression to every whimsical absurdity that his caprice dictates. And, as if that were not preposterous enough, he has forbidden me either to walk on my feet or to rise on the wings of poesy: I am a ridiculous cross between prose and verse; a monster of incongruity; a literary Centaur. (*Double Indictment* 33; cp. *The Fisherman* 26).[32]

Parody of mythic materials appears in several dialogues. Lucian's literary creativeness with respect to the plots and characters of traditional Greek myth had clear precedents: satyr plays, Old Comedy, and New Comedy. Satyr plays used the plots of traditional myths but had a comedic tone; Old Comedy transplanted gods to new contemporary settings; Lucian used both techniques.[33] From Old Comedy Lucian borrowed a focus on the most human elements of the gods, those that would most readily lend themselves to comical treatment such as the appetites or bodily functions (*Dialogues of the Gods; Dialogues of the Sea-Gods*).[34] In *Dialogues of the Gods*, for

32 Fowler translation, vol. 3.

33 Branham, *Unruly Eloquence*, 134–135.

34 Ibid., 143, 157. The parallels to Old Comedy in Lucian's dialogue and non-dialogue works are numerous. Athenian Comedy targeted deified humans and heroes (half-human, half-divine). For example, Heracles and Dionysus had risible traits permanently attached to them in the comic theater. Many comedies referenced Heracles' proverbial gluttony and amorous nature. Good examples of both can be found in Aristophanes' *Frogs* in which characters mistaken for Heracles are characterized as greedy and lustful, see lines 60–65; 503–507; 513–525; 549–560. Dionysus was often portrayed as a figure of ineptitude or cowardice (as in *Frogs* 280–310; 460–502). Extant titles or synopses of several plays suggest that the love

affairs of the gods were a standard theme. At least eleven Old Comedy play-wrights (Teleclides, Cratinus, Apollophanes, Archippus, Aristophanes, Crates, Hermippus, Nicochares, Platon, Polyzelos, Sannyrion) wrote about the affairs of Zeus. To all of these, we can compare Lucian's mockery of the gods in his *Dialogues of the Dead* in the dialogues between Diogenes and Alexander; Philip and Alexander; Diogenes and Heracles; *Dialogues of the Gods* in the dialogues between Zeus, Asclepius, and Heracles; *Zeus Rants* 12; *The Assembly of the Gods* 4–8. Old Comedy also mocked foreign or extreme rites (Cratinus, *Thracian Women*; Platon, *Adonis*; Nicophon, *Adonis*; Aristophanes, *Seasons*; Aristophanes, *Lysistrata* (on the rites for Adonis), Eupolis, *Dyers* (on the Thracian goddess)). Lucian did this as well (*Gout* 113–116; *Lucius* 35–41—if it is by Lucian; *On Sacrifices* 14–15; *Assembly of the Gods* 9–11; *Dialogues of the Gods*, dialogue between Aphrodite and Eros; *The Passing of Peregrinus*; *On the Syrian Goddess*; *Zeus Rants* 8; 13). Oracles and soothsayers were a regular theme in Old Comedy, the subject of plays by Ameipsias, Teleclides, Aristophanes, Magnes, Lysippus, Cephisodorus, Cratinus, and Theopompus, in which they were frequently ridiculed. Oracles are depicted negatively in Lucian (*Demonax* 37; *The Lover of Lies* 38–39; *Zeus Rants* 6; 20; 28; 30–31; 43; *Dialogues of the Dead*, dialogues between Menippus, Amphilochus, and Trophonius; Menippus and Tiresias; *Dialogues of the Gods*, dialogue between Hera and Leto; *Assembly of the Gods* 12; *Alexander the False Prophet*; *Peregrinus* was associated with oracles (Athenagoras, *A Plea for the Christians* 26)). Divination was subject to critique in the dialogues of Plato and Cicero and it was a topic among the Second Sophistic writers who were divided over the efficacy of oracles (Apollonius of Tyana accepts them and Philostratus is hotly defensive about his hero's ability to foresee the future in 1.2.2 and Apollonius is depicted as foretelling the future several times; Dio of Chrysostom's writings contain anti-oracle passages (*On Servants* 23–28)). Some traditional religious practices receive negative attention in Lucian. The work *On Sacrifices* begins with a comprehensive statement of contempt for the practices of sacrifice, procession, and feasts in honor of the gods (1; see also 12–13); the mythic portrayal of the gods is ridiculed (1–9); cult statues are ridiculed (11); for a different view, see Hall, *Lucian's Satire*, 194–220. For more on the relationship between Old Comedy and Lucian, see Ralph Rosen, "Lucian's Aristophanes: On Understanding Old Comedy in the Roman Imperial Period," in *Athenian Comedy in the Roman Empire*, eds. C. W. Marshall, and Tom Hawkins (New York: Bloomsbury Academic Press, 2016), 143) and Ian C. Storey, "Exposing Frauds: Lucian and Comedy," in *Athenian Comedy in the Roman Empire*, eds. C. W. Marshall, and Tom Hawkins (New York: Bloomsbury Academic Press, 2016), 163-181; Keith Sidwell, "The Dead Philosophers' Society: New Thoughts on Lucian's *Piscator* and Eupolis' *Demes*," in *A Lucian for Our Times*, ed., Adam Bartley (Newcastle: Cambridge Scholars Publishing, 2009),109–120.

example, Zeus curses Love for transforming him into so many different types of shapes and forms; he must win the women of earth by magic and then, once they see his true form, they fall out of love after all (dialogue between Eros and Zeus). Lucian also casts the gods into roles played by stock characters in New Comedy—the beleaguered husband, the desperate lover, the domineering matron, the lazy slave (*Dialogues of the Gods*; *Dialogues of the Sea-Gods*).[35]

Philosophy is a consistent theme in Lucian's works. As mentioned above, the protagonist of the dialogues is sometimes a Cynic or Skeptic speaker. Some of these philosophers are depicted as living a good and sensible life (Menippus, Diogenes, Demonax, Nigrinus).[36] But no school of philosophy is presented positively across all of his writings.[37] False philosophers, which are a major theme throughout Lucian's works, were a common theme in general in the Second Sophistic (see for example *The Fisherman* which distinguishes between true philosophers and poseurs in 31–38 and 40–52)[38] but more often Lucian simply rejects the practice of philosophy as a whole. *Hermotimus* rejects the notion that a life of virtue

---

35   Branham, *Unruly Eloquence*, 144.

36   For a discussion of such protagonists see Bartley, "Techniques of Composition," 361–362; Branham, *Unruly Eloquence*, 14–28, 52–57, 61–62; Stephen Halliwell, *Greek Laughter: A Study of Cultural Psychology from Homer to Early Christianity* (Cambridge: Cambridge University Press, 2008), 372–387; Reilhan, *Ancient Menippean Satire*, 39–48.

37   Cynics were critiqued in *Passing of Peregrinus* and *Runaways* as well as *Symposium*; see C. P. Jones, *Culture and Society in Lucian* (Cambridge, MA: Harvard University Press, 1986), 27–31 and Branham, *Unruly Eloquence*, 199.

38   For discussion, see Hall, *Lucian's Satire*, 190–191; good examples are in Plutarch, *Isis and Osiris* 352c; Dio Chrysostom, *On Philosophy* 7–10; Philostratus, *Apollonius of Tyana* 2.29.2. Akin to this is the sophist (elided with the orator). This figure retains very much the same features it had in the dialogues of Plato; sophists also appear in other Second Sophistic authors such as Dio Chrysostom (see *Olympic Discourse* 13 where sophists are associated with deception and concern for fees) and Plutarch (on which see Thomas A. Schmitz, "Plutarch and the Second Sophistic," in *A Companion to Plutarch*, ed. Mark Beck (Malden, MA: Wiley Blackwell, 2014), 34–41).

and happiness can only be obtained by those elite few who devote their whole lives to the pursuit of philosophy. Other works depict philosophers as pretentious and contentious hypocrites who can offer nothing of positive value (*Menippus, Icaromenippus, Symposium, Dialogues of the Dead, Philosophies for Sale, The Fisherman*, and *The Dream*).[39] We can compare Plato to Lucian in this: both reject traditional modes of knowledge but in Lucian's case, philosophy is included among those to be rejected. For him, philosophy is no more authoritative than rhetoric or religion (also targets of his dialogues). Lucian devotes *True Story* to exposing and exploring the false in authoritative types of writings.[40]

> Athletes and physical trainers do not limit their attention to the questions of perfect condition and exercise; they say there is a time for relaxation also—which indeed they represent as the most important element in training. I hold it equally true for literary men that af-

---

39   See also *Menippus* 4–5; *Symposium* is a parody of a Platonic symposium in which the guests are philosophers who are depicted as behaving in decidedly un-philosophic ways; in *True Story* the target is often philosophers (Aristoula Georgiadou, and David H. J. Larmour, *Lucian's Science Fiction Novel True Histories: Interpretation and Commentary* (Boston: Brill, 1998), 40–44); *Dialogues of the Dead* appeals to philosophers to stop their pointless brangling regarding the universe (dialogue between Diogenes and Pollux); the hypocrisy of philosophers is the subject in the dialogues between Charon and Hermes; Menippus and Aeacus; Menippus and Cerberus; in *The Ship* Lycinus laughs at philosophers (46); in *Icaromenippus* 5; 8–9; 20–21; 29–34 the philosophers are inconsistent and quarrelsome as well as being hypocrites; in *Philosophies for Sale* Zeus puts philosophers up for auction; in *The Fisherman* Lucian himself ("Frankness") stands trial for his denigration of the philosophers in *Philosophies for Sale*; in *The Dream* 18 Pythagoras has been reincarnated as a rooster and admits to making innovations for their own sake.

40   Georgiadou and Larmour, *Lucian's Science Fiction Novel*, 3; the theme of truth and falsehood is also found in Celsus and Dio Chrysostom (3–4); Karen níMheallaigh, *Reading Fiction with Lucian: Fakes, Freaks and Hyperreality* (Cambridge: Cambridge University Press, 2014), 207 demonstrates that Lucian explores "the fake, the hybrid and the memetic"; her work also explores Lucian's engagement with the expanding genre of fiction.

ter severe study they should unbend the intellect, if it is to come perfectly efficient to its next task.

The rest they want will best be found in a course of literature which does not offer entertainment pure and simple, depending on mere wit or felicity, but is also capable of stirring an educated curiosity—in a way which I hope will be exemplified in the following pages. They are intended to have an attraction independent of any originality of subject, any happiness of general design, any verisimilitude in the piling up of fictions. This attraction is in the veiled reference underlying all the details of my narrative; they parody the cock-and-bull stories of ancient poets, historians, and philosophers; I have only refrained from adding a key because I could rely upon you to recognize as you read. (1–2).[41]

This is a good way to understand Lucian's project overall. Specifically he undertakes to engage with and to mock the themes and methods of his contemporaries who gave such weight to the classical canon. He issues an intellectual, literary challenge to his readers.

As we have seen, the Second Sophistic authors were embarked on a process of self-definition. Through showing awareness of the canon and participating in a dialogue with that canon, Second Sophistic authors marked themselves as elite intellectuals in the best Greek tradition. And Lucian's writings, as Branham has put it, were intended to entertain these "traditionalists" of his day.[42] They are the ones who would recognize and appreciate what he was doing. His dialogue *The Dance*, for instance, is on the surface a defense of the Roman tradition of pantomime but the real point of the dialogue is to mock a traditional topic of philosophical discussion that goes back to Plato and is connected to Second Sophistic attempts to define and maintain Greek identity, the concept of serious play (Plato,

---

41 Fowler translation, vol. 2.

42 Branham, "Comic as Critic," 143.

Laws 7.803d–e).[43] The dialogue *Anacharsis* likewise engages with this same theme but also with the Second Sophistic interest in the Greek versus the barbarian (as its main speakers are the Scythian and an Athenian).[44] This theme is also present in *Toxaris* which also features a prototypical barbarian and a prototypical Greek. *Teacher of Rhetoric* and *Lexiphanes* mock the overuse of Atticisms (an over-reliance on the "pure" Attic language of the Archaic and Classical period).[45] *A Word with Hesiod* mocks the prophetic claims of this authoritative religious author.

Christian

We now move into the final group of dialogues that we will take up, the Christian dialogues. Just as Second Sophistic authors re-inscribed and sustained their identities as elite, educated Greeks by engaging with a canon, so too, did the early Christian communities. The Christian dialogues of course engage primarily with a different canon, the Hebrew Scriptures, and also, to varying degrees, the writings that make up today's New Testament, but they would also be influenced by the philosophical tradition and by the genre known as the apology.

The philosophical dialogue we have covered in some detail; the apologetic genre refers to a literary work that represents a defense or

---

43   "Athenian: At present they think that their serious pursuits should be for the sake of their sports, for they deem war a serious pursuit, which must be managed well for the sake of peace; but the truth is, that there neither is, nor has been, nor ever will be, either amusement or instruction in any degree worth speaking of in war, which is nevertheless deemed by us to be the most serious of our pursuits. And therefore, as we say, every one of us should live the life of peace as long and as well as he can. And what is the right way of living? Are we to live in sports always? If so, in what kind of sports? We ought to live sacrificing, and singing, and dancing, and then a man will be able to propitiate the Gods, and to defend himself against his enemies and conquer them in battle." (7.803d–e; Jowett translation, vol. 5)

44   Athletics and gymnasium (*Anacharsis*; discussed in Branham, *Unruly Eloquence*, 81–104.

45   Tim Whitmarsh, *The Second Sophistic* (Oxford: Oxford University Press for the Classical Association, 2005), 45–47.

explanation of a particular person, group, or cause. This genre was in use among Greeks, Jews, Romans, and Christians.[46] Christians found it a good medium through which to present themselves to the rest of the world. They needed to articulate how they were both like and unlike the cultures that surrounded them, pagan, and Jewish. The earliest Christian dialogues serve the same function. In content, they cover Christianity's relationship with Jews and pagans and endorse and celebrate a chaste Christian life. Justin's *Dialogue with Trypho* explains how Christians are different from Jews; a Latin dialogue, *Octavius*, by Minucius Felix (died c. 250 CE), which takes Cicero's *On the Nature of the Gods* as its model, contrasts Roman and Christian views. Methodius's (died c. 311 CE) *Symposium* is in the form of a sympotic dialogue. This dinner party is unique in that the participants are all women, virgins, who each take it in turn to define and exhort the merits of a life lived in Christian chasteness.[47]

In the following analysis of the first extant Christian dialogue, we consider here as we have before, audience, frame, and author versus persona. We attempt to read the work as a discrete text on its own terms and also to read it with regard to its genre predecessors, other works by Justin, and other early Christian writings from about the same time period with similar themes.

Dialogue with Trypho

What we know about Justin Martyr (lived 100–165 CE) comes primarily from his own extant writings which include two apologies in addition to his dialogue. In 1 *Apology* 1, Justin tells us that he is the son of Priscus, grandson of Bacchius from Flavia Neapolis in Syria Palestine. In *Trypho*, Justin states that Christ was born 150 years ago (1 *Apology* 46). *Trypho* is dedicated to one Marcus Pompeius (see 8 where the name is missing in the Greek but supplied in the Latin version and 141). The frame is a meeting in Ephesus after the recent

---

46   See Mark J. Edwards, Martin Goodman, and Simon Price, eds., *Apologetics in the Roman Empire: Pagans, Jews, and Christians*, in association with Christopher Rowland (Oxford: Clarendon Press, 1999).

47   On Methodius' *Symposium*, see König, *Saints and Symposiasts*, 151–176.

Bar Kokhba Revolt (for Ephesus see Eusebius, *History of the Church* 4.18.6; for the revolt see *Dialogue* 1 and 9; 1 *Apology* 31 and 47).

The dialogue begins with Trypho and Justin Martyr both establishing that they are familiar with philosophy (1). Then Justin proceeds to explain how his Christian views differ from philosophy (2–8). In 8–10, the main focus of the dialogue is introduced. Trypho advises Justin to go back to the Mosaic Law in order to secure his salvation and to reject the false notion of the Messiah that he now holds. In the rest of the dialogue, Justin undertakes to prove to Trypho the scriptural basis of his Christian beliefs.

Both the main speakers, Justin and Trypho, are characterized at the outset as philosophers and their dialogue as an exercise in philosophical exchange. Trypho hails Justin Martyr as a philosopher on account of his distinctive philosopher's dress (he wears the philosopher's cloak, the *pallium*) (1). Trypho shows himself to be eager for an exchange of views and reveals his own connection with, and interest in, philosophy: "I was instructed … by Corinthus the Socratic in Argos, that I ought not to despise or treat with indifference those who array themselves in this dress, but to show them all kindness, and to associate with them, as perhaps some advantage would spring from the intercourse either to some such man or to myself" (1).[48] Justin and Trypho agree that philosophy is the search for God (1). Having established that there is an affinity between some philosophical teachings and Christianity, a theme which is also present in Justin's apologies,[49] Justin now proceeds to stress the

---

48   All translations of this text are taken from *The Ante-Nicene Fathers, Translations of the Writings of the Fathers Down to A.D. 325*, eds. Alexander Roberts, James Donaldson, and A. Cleveland Coxe, vol. 1 (New York: Charles Scribner's Sons, 1913).

49   References to philosophy occur in all of Justin's works. Justin used philosophy as a way of introducing Christians to the Roman emperors. In his apologies, Justin addresses them as lovers of piety and philosophers (1 *Apology* 1; 2; 12). Justin seeks to demonstrate that good philosophers (such as Socrates and Plato) and Christians share the same core teachings—though Christianity in fact preceded philosophy (1 *Apology* 46; 59–60; 2 *Apology* 10).

differences. Justin states that his own philosophy is different from that of other philosophers and Trypho asks him to explain (1). This gives Justin the opportunity to describe how he moved from philosophy to Christianity.

In 3–8, Justin recounts his fateful encounter with a venerable old man who convinced him of the superiority of Christian teaching. In this section, the frame of the dialogue begins to shift from philosophical to scriptural. Justin first praises true philosophers as holy men and tells us that in the past he had studied with a Stoic, Peripatetic, and Pythagorean (2). In a dialogue within a dialogue, in a series of quick Q and A, Justin and the old man discuss some standard topics of philosophy (which occur in both Plato and Plutarch): how we can know God, can animals know God, and the transmigration of souls (3–7). Justin initially attempts to defend philosophers but the old man convinces Justin that these philosophers know nothing (3–5). He suggests that true knowledge comes from the prophets and that the only way to the Truth is through the enlightenment provided by Christ (7). This becomes the basis of Justin's new philosophy (8). In what follows, Justin lays out his Christian beliefs, attempting to justify them on the basis of Hebrew Scripture. In 11–141, three interrelated themes are taken up by Justin: the redundancy of Mosaic Law, the new covenant for Gentiles, and the Messiah foretold in the scriptures is the Christian Christ.

In 13–23, Justin takes up in succession the regulations of Mosaic Law and shows via scripture why it is no longer necessary to observe these.[50] Justin provides different reasons for the redundancy of Mosaic Law. The Law was given because the people were sinful (21–23) or in the case of circumcision, it was given to the Hebrews to mark them out for future punishment (16; 19; the idea is reflected in Tertullian, *Against the Jews* 3); elsewhere he states that the Mosaic Law was but a type or symbol of the true wishes of God (42; see also 14).

Trypho objects that Christ cannot be the Messiah because he does

---

50   Sacrifice (13); unleavened bread (14); circumcision (16).

not match the picture of the glorious Messiah found in the scripture. Justin begins his refutation in 32 to which he will return several times. His argument is that the scriptures refer to two different advents of the Messiah (or Christ). In the first advent, the Messiah will appear as a Suffering Servant; at the end of time he will return to the earth in glory (14; 31–32; 35; 40; 49; 52; 110; 111; there is a similar "two advents" interpretation in Tertullian, *Against the Jews* 14).

A challenge is issued to prove that Jesus of Nazareth is the one foretold by the prophecies relating to the Suffering Servant. Trypho concedes that the scripture may be interpreted as predicting a Suffering Servant but he is not convinced yet that Jesus is the one so indicated (36; 39). The dialogue ends with Trypho expressing his desire to keep talking and Justin's exhortation to believe in Christ and be saved.

The main interlocutor in the dialogue is Trypho, though other interlocutors (who accompanied him) are present and do occasionally interject (1; 85; 90; 94; 122). Trypho's Jewishness is central to the themes and aim of the dialogue. In this dialogue, Justin is not attempting to explain all of Christian teaching. He is rather only taking up those points of doctrine and practice that separated Christianity from Judaism (Christology, Mosaic Law). As an interlocutor, Trypho asks questions, makes counterarguments, and introduces fresh criticisms (see for example 8; 10; 25; 27; 35–36; 45; 67). Though he admits that some scriptural interpretations that Justin presents are plausible and at times concedes outright individual points, throughout he makes it clear that he is not being persuaded (28; 36; 39; 57; 67–68). At the end of the dialogue, he remains unconvinced, though he expresses his willingness to talk again (142).

The relationship between Trypho and Justin and the characterization of Trypho is inconsistent in the dialogue. Justin implies that Trypho and his companions (and by implication, the larger Jewish community) are truly convinced that he is correct and make objections only out of malice or a desire to be contrary (64–65; 67). This is reminiscent of the Platonic idea that the interlocutor must have the right kind of character in order to be able to benefit from the encounter. Such passages suggest that the dialogue is intended to serve as a condemnation of the Jewish community: they know the truth but will not admit it! Yet Trypho takes pains to wipe away this bad impression of himself. In 68, he responds to Justin's criticisms with a reasonable objection: "You endeavor to prove an incredible and well-nigh impossible thing." In 87, he is not being contentious, he says, but rather honestly asking for information. In 118 and then 123, he invites Justin to keep speaking, inviting him to rehash his arguments for the benefit of newcomers. The dialogue ends with expressions of good will on the part of Trypho and a desire to speak more. But Justin is leaving that very day. Justin's imminent departure indicates that further dialogue will not be possible. These factors imply that the function of the dialogue is not to show Christian readers how they might convert Jews. At the same time, the dialogue could well have ended with an angry rejection on the part of Trypho and the fact that his final words are amicable is perhaps meant as an incentive to Christian readers to not give up the good fight (as they might put it) but to continue the work of conversion. In 68, Trypho, who appears at this point to be all but convinced, says that he needs time to reflect on all that he has heard ("[Y]ou made yourself master of these [truths] with much labor and toil. And we accordingly must diligently scrutinize all that we meet with, in order to give our assent to those things which the Scriptures compel us [to believe]"). This also suggests that Justin intends his readers to see Jewish conversion as a real possibility.

The characterization of Trypho raises the issue of audience. Who was the intended reader of the dialogue? Regardless of whether one reads the dialogue as implying that Jewish conversion to Christianity is a possibility or thinks that Trypho is merely being condemned, it is most plausible to assume a Christian readership. While Jewish readers or pagan readers might have had an interest in learning what distinguishes Christians from Jews, only Christians would have an interest in either reading why Jews cannot be converted or in learning the types of arguments that might lead to their conversion.[51]

The exchanges in the dialogue are driven by the same type of competitive display that characterized the Second Sophistic authors. The focus is on the right reading of the shared tradition (who is doing it best?) but the tradition in this case is of the Jewish–Christian variety. Trypho and Justin accept the authority of the Hebrew Scriptures and particular attention is given to the writings of the prophets.[52] They are both also familiar with Christian teaching

---

51   Lawrence Lahey, "Evidence for Jewish Believers," in Christian–Jewish Dialogues through the Sixth Century (Excluding Justin)," in *Jewish Believers in Jesus: The Early Centuries*, eds. Oskar Skarsaune, and Reidar Hvalvik (Peabody, MA: Hendrickson Publishers, 2007), 585, 620–631. Compare Tessa Rajak, "Talking at Trypho: Christian Apologetic as Anti-Judaism in Justin's *Dialogue with Trypho the Jew*," in *Apologetics in the Roman Empire: Pagans, Jews, and Christians*, eds. Mark J. Edwards, Martin Goodman, and Simon Price, in association with Christopher Rowland (Oxford: Clarendon Press, 1999), 74–80. Rajak thinks that the touches of amiability at the beginning and end of the dialogue ring false. She reads the overall tone as vindictive, noting in particular Justin's accusation that the Jews practice systematic persecution and cursing of Christians (Justin Martyr, *Dialogue* 16–17; 47; 108); on Christian accusations of systematic persecution see 1 Corinthians 15:9; Galatians 1:13; Philippians 3:6; John 9:22; 12:42; *Martyrdom of Polycarp* 12.2; 13.1; 17.2; 18.1; Tertullian, *Against the Jews* 13.26; B. Sanhedrin 43a.

52   A stress on prophecy was also a way to connect with the Romans as divination was a part of their culture too and we can see Justin trying to appeal to the proof of prophecy in his 1 *Apology* 18; 20; 31–53 and we may mention here again the work of Johnston which notes the important role of prophecy in Greek and Roman culture (Johnston, *Ancient Greek Divination*, 4); for the role of prophecy in early Christian communities see Laura Nasrallah, *An Ecstasy of Folly: Prophecy and Authority in Early Christianity* (Cambridge, MA: Harvard University Press, 2004). In the *Dialogue*, prophets preceded philosophy (7; see also 1 *Apology* 23; 59–60); prophets are the only sure way to the truth (*Dialogue* 8); the gift of prophecy has passed from Jews to Christians (*Dialogue* 51; 82; 87); false prophets perform wonders and glorify demons (*Dialogue* 7). Demons are another recurring theme for Justin: demons and the Devil imitate scripture (*Dialogue* 69–70); the gods of the Gentiles are demons (*Dialogue* 83; cp. 1 *Apology* 5; 9; 12; 54; 64; 2 *Apology* 5). Justin attributes to these beings prevailing false conceptions of the gods (through poetry: 1 *Apology* 4; 21;

(Trypho has read the teachings of Jesus as we see in 18). Another key difference between this dialogue and other Second Sophistic texts is what is at stake. Justin believes—as he states very clearly at the beginning and end of the dialogue—that what is at stake are the souls of the interlocutors (8; 142). Adhering to wrong interpretation will result in incurring the wrath of God (115).

Justin reveals that some interpretive principles overlap for both groups. Both Jews and Christians, he says, believe that scripture does not contradict itself ("I am entirely convinced that no Scripture contradicts another," 65). Both groups believe that the prophets expressed themselves in "parables and types" (90). But the Jews, according to Justin, do not apply these methods correctly: they read the text literally when they should interpret nonliterally (14; 112; see also 42; 94). The interpretation of the serpent of bronze, raised up by Moses in the wilderness (Numbers 21:9; 2 Kings 18:4) is taken up by Justin in 94–97 and 112 (see also John 3:14; *Epistle of Barnabas* 12.5–7 and Tertullian, *Against the Jews* 10.10). This passage was puzzling to the Jewish interlocutors who accompanied Trypho (94). Justin derides the "foolish" interpretation which the Jewish teachers apply to this scripture and seeks to demonstrate that only a symbolic interpretation makes sense (112; see also 65 in which Justin corrects the interpretation of Isaiah 42:8).

For Justin the Jews are not just bad interpreters of the tradition. They also do not respect the received canon. Trypho asks about the Christian view of the Triune God and the virgin birth. How can Justin prove that there is another God besides the Creator and that this other God was born of a virgin (50)? Trypho objects that the scriptural prophecy that Justin puts forward is ambiguous and cannot be interpreted as Justin suggests (51). But Trypho also objects that Justin has used the wrong text: it is not a "virgin" who will conceive but a "young woman" (67; Isaiah 7:14). In this case, what

---

54; 2 *Apology* 5), the persecution of Christians (*Dialogue* 18; 1 *Apology* 57; 2 *Apology* 1; 8; 12), and heresies (1 *Apology* 26; 56, 58). For Justin, demons cause all sorts of wrong religious beliefs and actions (1 *Apology* 14; 25–26; 62).

is under contention is not only a different reading of the received text but a textual variant. Justin states that he is willing to confine their discussion to the same, agreed upon, text (71–72) but in fact he repeatedly draws attention to this question of textual variants, accusing the Jews of having tampered with the authoritative text of the scriptures.[53]

For Justin, the Septuagint, the Greek text of the Hebrew Scriptures produced, according to legend, by seventy Jewish scribes for Ptolemy II, represents the standard, the authoritative text. He accuses the Jewish teachers of having deleted portions of the Septuagint yet the scriptural quotations that he himself adduces as the correct readings rarely come from any known variants of the Septuagint.[54] Oskar Skarsaune has argued that Justin draws on Jewish and Jewish–Christian sources for his scriptural quotations.[55] Rajak, however, warns that there is a strong polemical tinge to this work so although the dialogue may allow us to reconstruct scriptural textual variants known to or used by early Christians, it cannot be used similarly for Jewish communities. Justin Martyr, in a sense, *must* prove that the Jewish community has changed the authentic text in order to support Christian claims to be the true heirs and guardians of God's Word. We cannot therefore take his word as to what texts Jewish communities were actually using or what motivations they may have had in creating or using textual variations.[56]

There is no evidence or reason to believe that this dialogue ever

---

53 On Isaiah 7:14 see also Tertullian, *Against the Jews* 9.2 in which passage Tertullian accuses the Jews of not reading the passage properly, according to its context.

54 See especially 43; 68; 71–73; 120; 124; 131; 137; 1 *Apology* 31.

55 For a thorough discussion of Justin Martyr's Septuagint variants and his sources, see Oskar Skarsaune, *The Proof from Prophecy: A Study in Justin Martyr's Proof-text Tradition: Text-type, Provenance, Theological Profile* (Leiden: Brill, 1987), *passim*, in particular 25–91 and "Jewish Christian Sources Used by Justin Martyr and Some Other Greek and Latin Fathers," in *Jewish Believers in Jesus: The Early Centuries*, eds. Oskar Skarsaune and Reidar Hvalvik (Peabody, MA: Hendrickson Publishers, 2007), 379–416.

56 Rajak, "Theological Polemic," 130–139.

took place; Trypho is an invented person.[57] This work, however, can still be used as evidence for how Christians tried to work out the relationship between Judaism and Christianity. Lawrence Lahey has provided a survey of dialogues from antiquity that depict Christian–Jewish debates or encounters.[58] One of these, *Dialogue of Jason and Papiscus*, predates Justin Martyr's *Dialogue with Trypho*. The work today is extant only in fragments and in summaries from ancient writers. These tell us that the Christian protagonist, Jason, was a Hebrew Christian and that he succeeded in converting his Jewish opponent, Papiscus, by dialogue's end (Celsus Africanus, *Letter to Vigilius Concerning Jewish Unbelief* 8). Origen, *Against Celsus* 4.52, tells us that in this work, Jason demonstrated to Papiscus, via the scriptures, that Jesus was the Messiah. We can see then that some of its arguments, as we might expect, were similar to Justin's.

Other works of this approximate period include themes similar to those found in Justin's dialogue in particular the *Epistle of Barnabas* and Tertullian's *Against the Jews* (which takes as its point of departure a debate between a Christian and a Jewish proselyte, 1). To take but two examples from these works, the *Epistle of Barnabas* also relies on scripture to establish the end of Mosaic Law (2.4–3.6; 9.1–10.12; 15.2–9) and supersessionism is evident throughout this work (but see especially 4.6–8, 14; 13.1–14.8; for supersessionism in the *Dialogue* see 11; 24–26; 29; 44; 121–125; 130–136; 139–140; prophecy is transferred to the Christians 51; 82; 87; those who believe in Christ are the new Israel 123–125; 130; 135; 1 *Apology* 49; 53). In Tertullian, *Against the Jews*, we see a similar concern to establish the redundancy of Mosaic Law (2–6) and a strong supersessionist message (1; 3; 6; 11–14). In Justin's view, the majority of Jews are going to reject Christ as was foretold in scriptures (*Dialogue* 120); Tertullian expresses the same idea (*Against the Jews* 11.11 and 13.28).

---

57   Rajak, "Talking at Trypho," 63–64, 69; "Theological Polemic and Textual Revision in Justin Martyr's *Dialogue with Trypho the Jew*," in *Greek Scripture and the Rabbis*, eds. Timothy Michael Law and Alison Salvesen (Walpole, MA: Peeters, 2012), 131.

58   Lahey, "Evidence for Jewish Believers," 581–639.

If we read *Dialogue with Trypho* in light of these contemporary works, we can see that Justin was taking part in an ongoing conversation about the relationship between the two faiths, Judaism and Christianity, and debates over how to evaluate the relationship of the Jewish people with God in light of the new covenant between God and the Gentiles. Trypho often asks Justin about the status of Jews with respect to salvation (both past and present). Justin is in line with his contemporaries in that he thinks that contemporary Jews, the race of Israel, no longer has a favored relationship with God.

What we witness in the dialogue are two different ways of defining Jewishness, one based, as Skarsaune puts it, on ideology (belief) and the other one based on ethnicity. When Trypho refers to "us" or Justin to "the descendants of Abraham" we can be pretty sure that ethnic Jews are what is meant.[59] But there were persons who believed that Jesus was the Messiah and who observed Mosaic Law—some of these were ethnically Jewish and some were Gentile born.[60] It is not always obvious which of these two groups are being referred to. In 64, Trypho suggests that perhaps ethnically born Jews will be saved via Mosaic Law, but Gentiles must be saved through belief in Christ. He proposes in effect two alternative routes to salvation based on ethnicity. Justin rejects this notion in no uncertain terms. He is convinced that contemporary Jews must accept Christ in order to be saved. Those who had lived in the pre-Christ world, however, if they had lived according to the Mosaic Law, would be saved and welcomed into the New Jerusalem (45; 80).

Justin himself seems to have been uncertain about the consequences for Christians (of whatever ethnicity) of observing Mosaic Law. The first time the issue is raised, Justin is rather laconic. Justin says

---

59   Compare the language of *Epistle of Barnabas* "ours" and "theirs" (4.6; see also 13.1–14.9).

60   Oscar Skarsaune, "Jewish Believers in Jesus in Antiquity—Problems of Definition, Method, and Sources," in *Jewish Believers in Jesus: The Early Centuries*, eds. Oskar Skarsaune, and Reidar Hvalvik (Peabody, MA: Hendrickson Publishers, 2007), 3–21.

that those who seek to justify themselves on the basis of their rela-tionship with Abraham (an ethnic categorization) will not inherit anything on the holy mountain. Trypho is surprised: What, will none of us inherit? Justin answers: I do not say that but certain-ly those who have persecuted the Christians shall not (if they do not repent; an ideological categorization) (25–26). The next time the issue is raised, Justin responds in the affirmative for those Jews who lived before Christ's advent (45). All the options for the rela-tionship between the Mosaic Law and Christian belief are brought forward for consideration in the dialogue (ethnic Jews who believe in Christ and also follow Mosaic Law; ethnic non-Jews who believe in Christ and follow Mosaic Law). If a man believes in Christ and also wants to observe the Mosaic Law he will be saved, according to Justin, provided that he try to convince no one else that the Law is necessary for salvation (46–47). The descendants of Abraham who do not believe in Christ or who previously believed in Christ but then recanted and returned to a sole reliance upon Mosaic Law (abjuring Christ) will not be saved (47). Justin refers to Christian heresies in the dialogue but in his view there can be more than one opinion about the validity of continued observance of Mosaic Law among those who believe in Christ; disagreement over this issue was allowable (47; 80; see 35; 80 for his remarks on outright heresies).

From the historian's point of view, *Dialogue with Trypho* would make an excellent source for second-century Christian ideas about Jews, Jewish–Christian relations, scriptural texts, and scriptural interpretation. We can also see in this work some of the recurring themes of the genre that date back to its inception: philosophy, religion, authority, and some of the same methods of operation through its interest in literary precedents and canonical texts. Justin's readers, like Plato's or Tacitus', would come to this text with the expectation that they were about to take part in a highly literary exercise, one that would require them to recognize and appreciate genre conventions, allusions, and manipulations of familiar texts.

Conclusion

Although we have seen authors across the centuries modify the dialogue form, the dialogues from Plato to Justin Martyr do share common themes. The dialogues we have surveyed make excellent sources for philosophy, religion, and literary culture. They share a strong interest in the reexamination or reinterpretation of authoritative traditions.

The dialogue in ancient Greece and Rome went through periods of popularity and decline but it was present from the classical period through late antiquity and carried over into medieval culture and Byzantine culture. For all ancient texts, historians ask who created it, when, and why? We try to determine the author's agenda and try to situate the text within its larger historical context. For the dialogue, we must do more than this. We must consider the conventions of the genre as well as earlier examples of the form. As we have seen, dialogists consciously engaged in a conversation with contemporary texts and with their predecessors in the genre. When we read ancient dialogues today, we must always recognize that we are reading texts that are "multitasking."

Translations

Aristotle. *Aristotle's Theory of Poetry and Fine Art with a Critical Text and Translation of The Poetics.* Translated by H. S. Butcher. Fourth edition. New York: Macmillan, 1920.

_____. *The Rhetoric of Aristotle.* Translated by J. E. C. Welldon. New York: Macmillan, 1886.

Cicero. *The Letters of Cicero.* Translated by Evelyn S. Shuckburgh. 4 vols. London: George Bell and Sons, 1900).

_____. *Cicero on Oratory and Orators.* Translated by J. S. Watson. New York: Harper & Brothers, 1875.

_____. *The Treatises of M. T. Cicero: On the Nature of the Gods; On Divination; On Fate; On the Republic; On the Laws; and On Standing for the Consulship.* Translated by C. D. Yonge. London: George Bell & Sons, 1878.

Diogenes Laertius. *The Lives and Opinions of Eminent Philosophers by Diogenes Laërtius.* Translated by C. D. Yonge. London: George Bell & Sons, 1853.

Justin Martyr. *The Ante-Nicene Fathers, Translations of the Writings of the Fathers Down to A.D. 325.* Edited by Alexander Roberts, James Donaldson, and A. Cleveland Coxe. 10 vols. New York: Charles Scribner's Sons, 1913.

Lucian of Samosata. *The Works of Lucian of Samosata.* Translated by H. W. Fowler and F. G. Fowler. 4 vols. Oxford Clarendon Press, 1905.

Philostratus. *The Life of Apollonius of Tyana, The Epistles of Apollonius and the Treatise of Eusebius.* Translated by F. C. Conybeare. 2 vols. London: William Heinemann; New York: Macmillan, 1912.

Plato. *The Dialogues of Plato*. Translated by Benjamin Jowett. Third edition. Oxford University Press, 1892.

Plutarch. *Plutarch's Morals*. Translated by William W. Goodwin. 5 vols. Boston: Little, Brown and Company, 1878.

Tacitus. *The Agricola and Germany of Tacitus and the Dialogue on Oratory*. Translated by Alfred John Church and William Jackson Brodribb. Revised edition. New York: Macmillan, 1899.

_____. *Annals of Tacitus*. Translated by Alfred John Church and William Jackson Brodribb. London: Macmillan, 1882.

Xenophon. *The Works of Xenophon*. Translated by H. G. Dakyns. 4 vols. New York: Macmillan, 1897.

BIBLIOGRAPHY

Ahbel-Rappe, Sara and Rachana Kamtekar, eds. *A Companion to Socrates*. Malden, MA: Blackwell, 2006.

Allison, J. "Tacitus' *Dialogus* and Plato's *Symposium*." *Hermes* 127 (1999): 479–492.

Anderson, Graham. "The Banquet of Belles-Lettres: Athenaeus and the Comic Symposium." In *Athenaeus and His World: Reading Greek Culture in the Roman Empire*, edited by David Braund and John Wilkins, 316–326. Foreword by Glen Bowerstock. Exeter: University of Exeter Press, 2000.

Ash, Rhiannon, ed. *Oxford Readings in Tacitus*. Oxford: Oxford University Press, 2012.

Asmis, Elizabeth. "Plato on Poetic Creativity." In *Cambridge Companion to Plato*, edited by Richard Kraut, 338–364. Cambridge: Cambridge University Press, 1992.

Bartley, Adam. "Techniques of Composition in Lucian's Minor Dialogues." *Hermes* 133.3 (2005): 358–67.

Bartsch, Shadi. "Praise and Doublespeak: Tacitus' *Dialogus*." In *Oxford Readings in Tacitus*, edited by Rhiannon Ash, 119-154. Oxford: Oxford University Press, 2012. Updated reprint of chapter 4 of *Actors in the Audience*. Cambridge, MA: Harvard University Press,1994.

Beck, Mark. *A Companion to Plutarch*. Malden, MA: Wiley Blackwell, 2014.

Benson, Hugh H. "Problems with the Socratic Method." In *Does Socrates Have a Method? Rethinking the Elenchus in Plato's Dialogues and Beyond*, edited by G. A. Scott, 101–113. University Park, PA: Penn State University Press, 2002.

_____, ed. *A Companion to Plato*. Malden, MA: Blackwell, 2006.

_____. "Plato's Method of Dialectic." In *A Companion to Plato*, edited by Hugh H. Benson, 85–99. Malden, MA: Blackwell, 2006.

Blondell, Ruby. *The Play of Character in Plato's Dialogues*. Cambridge: Cambridge University Press, 2002.

Boyarin, Daniel. *Border Lines: The Partition of Judaeo-Christianity*. Philadelphia: University of Pennsylvania Press, 2004.

Branham, Bracht R. "The Comic as Critic: Revenging Epicurus: A Study of Lucian's Art of Comic Narrative." *Classical Antiquity* 3.2 (1984): 143–163.

_____. *Unruly Eloquence: Lucian and the Comedy of Traditions*. Cambridge, MA: Harvard University Press, 1989.

Braund, David and John Wilkins, eds. *Athenaeus and His World: Reading Greek Culture in the Roman Empire*. Foreword by Glen Bowerstock. Exeter: University of Exeter Press, 2000.

Carpenter, Michelle and Ronald M. Polansky. "Variety of Socratic Elenchi." In *Does Socrates Have a Method? Rethinking the Elenchus in Plato's Dialogues and Beyond*, edited by G. A. Scott, 89–100. University Park, PA: Penn State University Press, 2002.

Desjardins, Rosemary. "Why Dialogues? Plato's Serious Play." In *Platonic Writings/Platonic Readings*, edited by Charles L. Griswold, 110–126. University Park, PA: Pennsylvania State University Press, 1988.

Dillon, John. "Plutarch and Platonism." In *A Companion to Plutarch*, edited by Mark Beck, 61–72. Malden, MA: Wiley Blackwell, 2014.

Edwards, Mark J., Martin Goodman, and Simon Price, eds. *Apologetics in the Roman Empire: Pagans, Jews, and Christians.* In association with Christopher Rowland. Oxford: Clarendon Press, 1999.

Fine, Gail, ed. *The Oxford Handbook of Plato.* Oxford: Oxford University Press, 2008.

Flower, Michael. *The Seer in Ancient Greece.* Berkeley: University of California Press, 2008.

Ford, Andrew. "The Beginnings of Dialogue: Socratic Discourses and Fourth-Century Prose." In *The End of Dialogue in Antiquity*, edited by Simon Goldhill, 29–44. Cambridge: Cambridge University Press, 2008.

Fortenbaugh, William W. *Theophrastean Studies.* Stuttgart: Franze Steiner Verlag, 2003.

Frede, Michael. "Plato's Arguments and the Dialogue Form." In *Methods of Interpreting Plato and his Dialogues*, edited by James C. Klagge and Nicholas D. Smith, 201–219. Oxford: Clarendon Press, 1992.

_____. "The Literary Form of the Sophist." In *Form and Argument in Late Plato*, edited by Christopher Gill and Mary Margaret McCabe, 135–151. Oxford: Clarendon Press, 1996.

Freydberg, Bernard. *Philosophy & Comedy: Aristophanes, Logos, and Erōs.* Indiana: Indiana University Press, 2008.

Gallia, Andrew. "*Potentes* and *Potentia* in Tacitus's *Dialogus de oratoribus.*" *Transactions of the American Philological Association* 139 (2009):169–206.

Gill, Christopher and Mary Margaret McCabe, eds. *Form and Argument in Late Plato.* Oxford: Clarendon Press, 1996.

_____. "Afterword: Dialectic and the Dialogue Form in Late Plato." In *Form and Argument in Late Plato*, edited by Christopher

Gill and Mary Margaret McCabe, 283–311. Oxford: Clarendon Press, 1996.

_____. "Dialectic and the Dialogue Form." In *New Perspectives on Plato, Modern and Ancient*, edited by Julia Annas and Christopher J. Rowe, 149–161. Cambridge, MA: Harvard University Press, 2002.

Georgiadou, Aristoula and David H. J. Larmour. *Lucian's Science Fiction Novel True Histories: Interpretation and Commentary*. Boston: Brill, 1998.

Goldhill, Simon, ed. *The End of Dialogue in Antiquity*. Cambridge: Cambridge University Press, 2008.

_____. "Introduction: Why Don't Christians Do Dialogue?" In *The End of Dialogue in Antiquity*, edited by Simon Goldhill, 1–12. Cambridge: Cambridge University Press, 2008.

Hall, Jennifer. *Lucian's Satire*. Revised edition. New York: Arno Press, 1981.

Halliwell, Stephen. *Greek Laughter: A Study of Cultural Psychology from Homer to Early Christianity*. Cambridge/New York: Cambridge University Press, 2008.

Harrison, Stephen, ed. *A Companion to Latin Literature*. Oxford: Blackwell, 2005.

Hirsch-Luipold, Rainer. "Religion and Myth." Translated by Mark Beck. In *Companion to Plutarch*, edited by Mark Beck, 163–176. Malden, MA: Wiley Blackwell, 2014.

Irwin, T. H. "Plato: The Intellectual Background." In *Cambridge Companion to Plato*, edited by Richard Kraut, 51–89. Cambridge: Cambridge University Press, 1992.

Janaway, Christopher. "Plato and the Arts." In *A Companion to Plato*, edited by Hugh H. Benson, 388–400. Malden, MA: Blackwell, 2006.

Johnston, Sarah Isles. *Ancient Greek Divination*. Malden, MA: Wiley-Blackwell, 2008.

Jones, C. P. *Culture and Society in Lucian*. Cambridge, MA: Harvard University Press, 1986.

Kahn, Charles H. "Aeschines or Socratic Eros." In *The Socratic Movement*, edited by Paul A. Vander Waerdt, 87–106. Ithaca, NY: Cornell University Press, 1994.

Kamtekar, Rebecca. "Plato on Education and Art." In *Oxford Handbook of Plato*, edited by Gail Fine, 336–359. Oxford: Oxford University Press, 2008.

König, Jason. *Saints and Symposiasts: The Literature of Food and the Symposium in Greco Roman and Early Christian Culture*. Cambridge: Cambridge University Press, 2012.

Kraut, Richard, ed. *The Cambridge Companion to Plato*. Cambridge: Cambridge University Press, 1992.

Lahey, Lawrence. "Evidence for Jewish Believers in Christian-Jewish Dialogues through the Sixth Century (Excluding Justin)." In *Jewish Believers in Jesus: The Early Centuries*, edited by Oskar Skarsaune and Reidar Hvalvik, 581–639. Peabody, MA: Hendrickson Publishers, 2007.

Leigh, Matthew. "Oblique Politics: Epic of the Imperial Period. In *Literature in the Greek and Roman Worlds: A New Perspective*, edited by Oliver Taplin, 468–491. Oxford: Oxford University Press, 2000.

Lesher, James H. "Parmenidean *Elenchos*." In *Does Socrates Have a Method? Rethinking the Elenchus in Plato's Dialogues and Beyond*, edited by G. A. Scott, 19–35. University Park, PA: Penn State University Press, 2002.

Lévy, Carlos. "Cicero and the New Academy." In *The Cambridge*

History of Philosophy in Late Antiquity, edited by Loyd P. Garson. Vol. 1.Cambridge: Cambridge University Press, 2010. Kindle edition.

Lightfoot, J. L. ed. *Lucian. On the Syrian Goddess*. Oxford: Oxford University Press, 2003.

Long, A. A. "Plato and Hellenistic Philosophy." In *A Companion to Plato*, edited by Hugh H. Benson, 418–433. Malden, MA: Blackwell, 2006.

Luce, T. J. and A. J. Woodman, eds. *Tacitus and the Tacitean Tradition*. Princeton, NJ: Princeton University Press, 1993.

_____. "Reading and Response in the *Dialogus*." In *Tacitus and the Tacitean Tradition*, edited by T. J. Luce and A. J. Woodman, 11–38. Princeton, NJ: Princeton University Press, 1993.

MacKendrick, Paul. With the collaboration of Karen Lee Singh. *The Philosophical Books of Cicero*. New York: St. Martin's Press, 1989.

McCabe, Mary Margaret. "Form and the Platonic Dialogues." In *A Companion to Plato*, edited by Hugh H. Benson, 39–54. Malden, MA: Blackwell, 2006.

McPherran, Mark L. "Platonic Religion." In *A Companion to Plato*, edited by Hugh H. Benson, 244–259. Malden, MA: Blackwell, 2006.

Mikalson, Jon D. *Greek Popular Religion in Greek Philosophy*. Oxford: Oxford University Press, 2010.

Modrak, Deborah K. W. "Plato: A Theory of Perception or a Nod to Sensation? In *A Companion to Plato*, edited by Hugh H. Benson, 133–145. Malden, MA: Blackwell, 2006.

Morgan, Michael L. "Plato and Greek Religion." In *Cambridge Companion to Plato*, edited by Richard Kraut, 227–247. Cambridge: Cambridge University Press, 1992.

Nails, Debra. "The Life of Plato of Athens." In *A Companion to Plato*, edited by Hugh H. Benson, 1–12. Malden, MA: Blackwell, 2006.

Nasrallah, Laura. *An Ecstasy of Folly: Prophecy and Authority in Early Christianity*. Cambridge, MA: Harvard University Press, 2004.

Ní Mheallaigh, K. *Reading Fiction with Lucian: Fakes, Freaks and Hyperreality*. Cambridge: Cambridge University Press, 2014.

Nightingale, Andrea Wilson. *Genres in Dialogue: Plato and the Construct of Philosophy*. Cambridge: Cambridge University Press, 1995.

Powell, J. G. F. "Dialogues and Treatises." In *A Companion to Latin Literature*, edited by Stephen Harrison, 223–240. Oxford: Blackwell, 2005.

Prior, William J. "The Socratic Problem." In *A Companion to Plato*, edited by Hugh H. Benson, 25–35. Malden, MA: Blackwell, 2006.

Rajak, Tessa. "Talking at Trypho: Christian Apologetic as Anti-Judaism in Justin's *Dialogue with Trypho the Jew*." In *Apologetics in the Roman Empire*: *Pagans, Jews, and Christians*, edited by Mark Edwards, Martin Goodman, and Simon Price. In association with Christopher Rowland, 59–80. Oxford: Clarendon Press, 1999.

_____. "Theological Polemic and Textual Revision in Justin Martyr's *Dialogue with Trypho the Jew*." In *Greek Scripture and the Rabbis*, Timothy Michael Law and Alison Salvesen, eds., 127-140. Walpole, MA: Peeters, 2012.

Relihan, Joel C. *Ancient Menippean Satire*. Baltimore: Johns Hopkins University Press, 1993.

Romeri, Luciana. "The λογόδειπνον: Athenaeus between Banquet and Anti-Banquet." Translated by Kerensa Pearson. In *Ath-*

enaeus and His World, edited by David Braund and John Wilkins, 256–271. Foreword by Glen Bowerstock. Exeter: University of Exeter Press, 2000.

Rosen, Ralph. "Lucian's Aristophanes: On Understanding Old Comedy in the Roman Imperial Period." In *Athenian Comedy in the Roman Empire*, edited by C. W. Marshall and Tom Hawkins, 141–162. New York: Bloomsbury Academic Press, 2016.

Rowe, Christopher. "Interpreting Plato." In *A Companion to Plato*, edited by Hugh H. Benson, 13–24. Malden, MA: Blackwell, 2006.

_____. *Plato and the Art of Philosophical Writing*. Cambridge/New York: Cambridge University Press, 2007.

Rutledge, Steven H. *Imperial Inquisitions: Prosecutors and Informants from Tiberius to Domitian*. London: Routledge, 2001.

Saunders, Trevor J. "Plato's Later Political Thought." In *Cambridge Companion to Plato*, edited by Richard Kraut, 464–492. Cambridge: Cambridge University Press, 1992.

Sayre, Kenneth M. *Plato's Literary Garden: How to Read a Platonic Dialogue*. Notre Dame, IN: University of Notre Dame Press, 1995.

Schmitz, Thomas A. "Plutarch and the Second Sophistic." In *A Companion to Plutarch*, edited by Mark Beck, 32–42. Malden, MA: Wiley Blackwell, 2014.

Schofield, Malcolm. "Ciceronian Dialogue." In *The End of Dialogue in Antiquity*, edited by Simon Goldhill, 63–84. Cambridge: Cambridge University Press, 2008.

Scott, Gary Alan, ed. *Does Socrates Have a Method? Rethinking the Elenchus in Plato's Dialogues and Beyond*. University Park, PA: Penn State University Press, 2002.

Sedley, David. "Three Platonist Interpretations of the *Theaetetus*." In *Form and Argument in Late Plato*, edited by Christopher Gill and Mary Margaret McCabe, 79–103. Oxford: Clarendon Press, 1996.

Sidwell, Keith. "The Dead Philosophers' Society: New Thoughts on Lucian's *Piscator* and Eupolis' *Demes*." In *A Lucian for Our Times*, edited by Adam Bartley, 109–120. Newcastle: Cambridge Scholars Publishing, 2009.

Skarsaune, Oskar. *The Proof from Prophecy*: *A Study in Justin Martyr's Proof-text Tradition*: *Text-type, Provenance, Theological Profile*. Leiden: Brill, 1987.

_____. and Reidar Hvalvik, eds. *Jewish Believers in Jesus*: *The Early Centuries*. Peabody, MA: Hendrickson Publishers, 2007.

_____. "Jewish Believers in Jesus in Antiquity—Problems of Definition, Method, and Sources." In *Jewish Believers in Jesus*: *The Early Centuries*, edited by Oskar Skarsaune and Reidar Hvalvik, 3–21. Peabody, MA: Hendrickson Publishers, 2007.

_____. "Jewish Christian Sources Used by Justin Martyr and Some Other Greek and Latin Fathers." In *Jewish Believers in Jesus*: *The Early Centuries*, edited by Oskar Skarsaune and Reidar Hvalvik, 379–416. Peabody, MA: Hendrickson Publishers, 2007.

Steel, C. E. W. *Cicero, Rhetoric, and Empire*. Oxford: Oxford University Press, 2001.

Storey, Ian C. "Exposing Frauds: Lucian and Comedy." In *Athenian Comedy in the Roman Empire*, edited by C. W. Marshall and Tom Hawkins, 163–181. New York: Bloomsbury Academic Press, 2016.

Swain, Simon. "Defending Hellenism: Philostratus, *In Honour of Apollonius*." In *Apologetics in the Roman Empire*: *Pagans, Jews, and Christians*, edited by Mark J. Edwards, Martin Goodman,

Simon Price. In association with Christopher Rowland, 157–196. Oxford: Clarendon Press, 1999.

Taplin, Oliver, ed. *Literature in the Greek and Roman Worlds: A New Perspective*. Oxford: Oxford University Press, 2000.

Tarrant, Harold. "*Elenchos* and *Exetasis*: Capturing the Purpose of Socratic Interrogation." In *Does Socrates Have a Method? Rethinking The Elenchus In Plato's Dialogues and Beyond*, edited by G. A. Scott, 61–77. University Park, PA: Penn State University Press, 2002.

Van den Berg, Christopher S. *The World of Tacitus'* Dialogus de Oratoribus: *Aesthetics and Empire in Ancient Rome*. Cambridge: Cambridge University Press, 2014.

Van der Stockt, L. *Twinkling and Twilight*: *Plutarch's Reflections on Literature*. Brussels: Paleis der Academiën, 1992.

Van Nuffelen, Peter. *Rethinking the Gods*: *Philosophical Readings of Religion in the Post Hellenistic Period*. Cambridge University Press, Cambridge, 2011.

Versnel, H. S. *Coping with the Gods*: *Wayward Readings in Greek Theology*. Leiden; Boston: Brill, 2011.

Whitmarsh, Tim. *Greek Literature and the Roman Empire: The Politics of Imitation*. Oxford: Oxford University Press, 2001.

_____. *The Second Sophistic*. Oxford: Oxford University Press for the Classical Association, 2005.

Wilkins, John. "Dialogue and Comedy: The Structure of the *Deipnosophistae*." In *Athenaeus and His World*: *Reading Greek Culture in the Roman Empire*, edited by David Braund and John Wilkins, 23–37. Foreword by Glen Bowerstock. Exeter: University of Exeter Press, 2000.

Young, Charles M. "The Socratic Elenchus." In *A Companion to Plato*, edited by Hugh H. Benson, 55–69. Malden, MA: Blackwell, 2006.

www.ingramcontent.com/pod-product-compliance
Lightning Source LLC
Chambersburg PA
CBHW060024050426
42448CB00012B/2862